THE WAY I SAW IT

Nickey Rackard leads Wexford to hurling glory

by

Martin Codd

Published by Corrigeentee Publishing, Corrigeen,
Rathnure, Enniscorthy, Co. Wexford, Ireland.
Tel: 00 353 (0)86 8411451
Email: info@martincodd.com
Website: www.martincodd.com

ISBN No.: 0-9550886-1-5 - Hardback Edition
ISBN No.: 0-9550886-0-7

Front Cover Photograph: Nickey Rackard, courtesy *'Free Press'*

Back Cover Photograph: Courtesy P.A. Crane Collection, Ibar Carty.
This photograph was taken on 12 November 1961 by photographer Pat Crane of
the County Wexford Senior Hurling Championship Final, played in Gorey between
Enniscorthy St. Aidan's and Rathnure. In foreground are Bobby Rackard and Nick
O'Donnell. The photo probably says as much about the photographer as it does
about hurling, as he captures the style and grace of these two great players. Both
men were selected on the Team of the Millennium. Other players in the photo are:
Pat Morrissey, Syl Barron, Paddy Ryan, Murt Ryan (Rathnure), Ted Morrissey, Jim
Morrissey, Gerry Doyle (St. Aidan's).

Editors: **Pat Codd, Martin Codd Jnr., Mark Codd.**

Cover Design: **hopewire.**

Printed by: **C & R Print. 054-35295.**

List of Contents

Dedication

I dedicate this book to my wife Kitty.
We have walked the road of life
together since we were seventeen;
it has been a beautiful journey.

The author would like to thank all those who contributed photographs and other material for use in this book.
While considerable effort has been made to locate all holders of copyright to photographs in this book, we have been unable to contact some of these.

Thanks to Agnes Codd and Nick Hayes, Image Studio for sourcing photographs and additional work to cover photographs.

Thanks to Joeleen, Karen and Bernie for deciphering 560 pages of my handwriting.

Thanks to all my family for their support while I was writing this book.

Foreword

Martin has gathered, preserved and minded for us a treasure of memories from the Golden Age of Hurling in Wexford. He enters fully his memories in a way which brings together the collective memories of a county, a nation and a generation for whom hurling was a source of immense joy and rivalry. It has been factually recorded in many a GAA year book but we were missing a very important piece of the jigsaw - how it felt from inside the team over that long period before victory became sweet. Even though he describes the local, are we not drawn to reflect on the universal need for passion, drive, humour, excitement, hero worship, pride, failure, role modeling, physical and mental strength and ultimate victory? That the inside story of how 15-20 men set a county and country alight with excitement for a short period could have gone unrecorded is unthinkable! I have no doubt that the people who saw those matches will relive that same frisson of excitement.

From his first day at school at five, hurl in hand, to Wexford's All-Ireland victory in Croke Park in 1955, Martin enthralls us with a myriad of charm - filled stories of a young boy/man for whom hurling runs parallel to Kitty and family as the two most important loves of his life.

Many of us who are not of that generation have often been regaled with glorious accounts of certain scores or matches but the "full picture" was often missing. We are taken almost chronologically through every game from 1949-1956 and great credit is due to the writing for generating excitement instead of boredom in recounting those games. These stories are interspersed with some priceless anecdotes of how the winters were spent "doing ten or twelve hours a night catching rabbits and wood pigeons and selling them for the

English market," the aim being to get tough and skillful for the hurling season in the Spring. Who would have ever guessed that "rabbit lamping" would suffice as training for a future Wexford champion hurler! Who could forget the "traveling circus" i.e. hackney drivers who accompanied the team to various matches, or John Randall the master craftsman who crafted each hurl to suit each player. What about John Coady the local tailor in Rathnure who had to get help from outside the county to contend with the number of new suits needed for the first Sunday in September 1956?

We discover that victory finally came to this team when their confidence had slowly built over the years instilling a self-belief and a knowing that their time had come to claim the McCarthy cup. The question poses itself as to why victory did not come sooner. Martin conveys the sheer exhilaration of bringing such pride back to Wexford and to the local club, Rathnure.

This book made me laugh, as apart from some familiarity with the subject matter I was tickled pink at the innocence, the genuineness, the wit, the pathos, the creativity of a generation which had very little creature comforts but for whom our National Game was the light of their lives.

As a daughter of one of three brothers playing on this amazing team, I feel personally indebted to Martin, a man of great heart and soul, for recording for posterity with such love and skill, the memorable feelings of this great hurling era.

Marion Rackard

Introduction

Martin Codd has put pen to paper to record his personal account of the revival of the ancient game of hurling in County Wexford midway through the last century. He moves back and forth through the years and shows how memory can colour experience. His writing, which springs from the rich store of incidents resulting from his personal involvement in the period, recalls the glory days of Wexford hurling. They are memories from a world which has now all but disappeared. It was the end of the age of paraffin oil and candles; rural electrification, coincidentally with hurling, was about to light up the Wexford countryside.

Martin comes from a countryside of sturdy people, sheltered by the Blackstairs Mountain and watered by the River Boro. Patrick Kennedy, in his book "The Banks of the Boro", wrote, in 1856, of Martin's homeland - "Still to the west beyond and to the right lay the townlands of Rathnure, Coolbawn and Forrestalstown; on the horizon stretched the White Mountain ridge and the eminence of Cahir Rua's Den, and on the extreme right the lofty rugged mass of Mount Leinster." Being a farmer Martin knows the countryside intimately and is attuned to its pulse.

He vividly captures the social history of the period shortly after World War Two, when people lived frugally and the Celtic Tiger was still a long way off. The success of the Wexford hurling team in the nineteen fifties brought about a whole new experience for many people. With touching anecdotes he writes not only of his teammates and their endeavours in pursuit of the elusive All-Ireland title, but also of their supporters who travelled by bike, pony and trap, car, scut-lorry, bus and train. For a few glorious years Wexford hurling supporters were gallivanting all over the country.

By starting at the beginning of the story in 1949, the chronological progression through the years of striving and then success is well captured and might be an inspiration to others in "football" counties struggling to foster hurling today. The book treats us to the build-up of excitement throughout the county, the dramatic increase in the numbers attending the games, the Gaelic scribes in the National Press taking the Wexford team to their hearts by extolling their virtues and manliness, and the support of neutrals from other counties. The reader stands with them in Corrigan Park, Belfast, when the freezing temperature was tempered by the patriotic heat engendered by Paul Robeson's singing. He conveys the emotion and excitement of the great victories in the League and the Oireachtas Competition and the All-Ireland Victories of 1955 and 1956. It is history now, but the memory is fresh and the emotion is still near the surface.

Martin Codd's gentle nature is discernible throughout his story. Methinks he is too modest. He states he wasn't a great hurler, but a good one who loved the game. There is no expression of bitterness, no chip-on-the-shoulder syndrome shining through the narrative, no disclosure of a hostile attitude towards authority; just an honest account by a man who loved hurling and was an active participant during that most stirring period of Wexford's sporting history.

He always believed that everyone did their best for the cause. He is convinced that if a professional attitude existed at the time, Wexford would have won an All-Ireland title before 1955 and possibly would have won three or four in all. Nickey Rackard was his idol, both as a leader and as an inspiring teammate on the field. The rousing exhortations from Nickey during many dressing-room intervals add enormously to the human interest aspect of the book.

Martin Codd still lives in his beloved Askinfarney, surrounded by good people, fertile fields and a beautiful landscape 'neath the foothills of the Blackstairs and the White Mountain'.

Seán Doyle.

The Way I Saw It

Early in November 1949 I got a post card telling me I had been selected to play centerfield for the Wexford senior hurling team. The game, against Dublin, was in Croke Park, and I think it was in the National League. Dublin at that time was a big force in hurling, so, for me this was going to be a big, big occasion. I had never been to Croke Park, and only twice had I been to Dublin.

Wexford was then a leading football county, and its hurlers were looked on by outsiders as robust, with great spirit but very little skill. If someone said at the time that the county would win three All-Ireland senior hurling titles in the next eleven years, they would have been sent to that big old building outside Enniscorthy commonly referred to as 'the asylum'. But that is just what happened and, while my memory works for me, I'll tell the full story as I saw it.

Having played for the county over a period of sixteen years, from November 1949 until the All-Ireland final of 1965, I was involved with many different players and officials. When I look back and compare my commitment to the game then to what county players are asked to give today, I think the GAA as an amateur sporting organisation, is losing the plot. Never did I feel under pressure to train, or to live my life in a different way, as players are expected to do nowadays. Although I was involved in a few All-Ireland finals and a few National League finals, I would never class myself as a great player: I was a good hurler who loved to play. I was like a card player who was dealt a reasonably good hand when he was born, and I have tried to play those cards well.

To appreciate the Wexford senior hurling team of the 1950s, you would have to start about 1940 when Wexford reached the All-Ireland semi-final in junior hurling, only to be beaten by Cork. Nickey Rackard, at the age of eighteen years, was one of three players from the Rathnure club who played in that game; and, as Rathnure had won the county junior hurling championship that year, there was a whole new interest in the game at our school.

Since there was no underage championship at that time, except minor, some older boys attending secondary school in Enniscorthy used to organise games between fellows from our parish and neighbouring parishes. There were junior teams in these parishes, but they would have no involvement in our activities. The games I remember best were played in a field at the back of Floods' house in Castleboro, in Cloughbawn parish. It was there I first met Padge Kehoe, Martin Flood and his brother Tim. You got to those games as best you could. If you had a bike you were lucky; if not you walked across the fields, a journey of six or seven miles from Rathnure, but only two miles from my home. Out of these games came nine players who were on the Wexford team in 1956.

My father and some of the older men in the neighbourhood used to talk about the great Wexford football team of 1915-18, winners of four All-Irelands in a row, and of the hurlers who won the All-Ireland in 1910. Most of that team came from the other side of the county, east of the Slaney river, the area referred to as "across the water", from places such as Ballymurn, Blackwater, Screen and Castlebridge, which were the hurling strongholds then, but football later, became the dominant game in the county.

Wexford was again very strong at football in the 1940s and had won the Leinster championship in '45, but Wexford hurling was still a bit of a joke. In the Enniscorthy district, however, the game was gaining strength; Rathnure advanced to senior status in 1940, as did Enniscorthy St. Aidan's in 1945 and Cloughbawn in 1946. By 1946, when St. Aidan's

Wexford Senior Football Team
All-Ireland Senior Football Semi-Final, 1945.
Back row (from left): Sid Bluett, Jimmy Coady, Willie Kielthy,
Nicky Rackard, Fr. Dermot Clancy, Des O'Neill, Paddy Kehoe,
Joe Nolan, John O'Connor, J. Lacey, Mick Kehoe, Sean Eustace,
Stephen Roche, Co. Secretary. Front: Jackie Culleton, Ger
Kavanagh (Andrew Holden, Mascot on his knee), Tim O'Leary,
Tom Somers, John Morris, Jim Foley, Tom Doyle, Michael Hanlon.
On ground: Willie Goodison, Jimmie Murphy.
Cavan 1-4, Wexford 0-5.

and Rathnure first met in the county senior hurling final,
things were changing, with big crowds turning out for games,
and the standard of hurling improving all the time. There
were good teams in Horeswood, Ferns, New Ross and
Piercestown, but St. Aidan's, Rathnure and Cloughbawn
were dominant, being the only clubs to win the county senior
championship between 1946 and 1959.

The first time I saw a Wexford county team hurling was in
Enniscorthy in '48, when Dublin beat them in the
championship, but I don't remember much about the match.
As football was the game to follow at the time, I had travelled
to Carlow, a journey of thirty-five miles on my bicycle, to see
the footballers play Kildare and Offaly, and I remember those
games well.

My first spark of interest in the county hurling team was
in October '49 when Wexford played the All-Ireland

champions, Tipperary, in a League match in Wexford Park. Rathnure had two or three players on the team that day, but my big interest was in a young fellow by the name of Jim Morrissey. Jim was from a junior club in Camross and had got a great write-up in the local press after his performance in Wexford's previous game, in which he had made his debut. He was described as being a raw young lad, six feet tall, with a head of black hair, who could strike a ball overhead or on the ground and drive it a long distance. He showed no fear or nerves. I had two inches in height on Jim, but otherwise I thought I could fit the description. At half time in the match I went in on the pitch to have a look at the players - they didn't go back to the dressing rooms at half time in those days. I walked around Jim and had a good look at him and, as the youth of today would say, he looked "cool".

I had a good look at some of the Tipperary team, too. I recognised many of them from seeing their photos in the papers after the All-Ireland final of that year: Pat Stakelum, Seamus Bannon, Phil Shanahan, Tommy Doyle, Jimmy Kennedy, the Ryans and the Kennys, a great team who won

Our family, 1946, with our parents Martin and Agnes.
Back: Rita, Mark, Pat and Martin. Front, John, Tom and Vincent.

three All-Irelands in a row. It was my first time to see a really good hurling team, and I was impressed.

What pleased me most about the day was how Bobby Rackard held his own in this company. As I came home on my bike, a journey of twenty miles on an empty stomach, I recalled all the times I had played on Bobby in the schoolyard and the local hurling field, and I thought to myself, I could mix it with these fellows, too. The quality of the hurling that day impressed me so much that I wanted to be part of it - the speed of their striking amazed me. I had been hurling from the time I was five years of age, and loved it. I had brought a hurl to school on my first day and on every single day until I left at the age of thirteen.

In the summer of '49 I got my place as a corner back on the Rathnure senior hurling team for the county semi-final and again for the final, in which Cloughbawn beat us. I played on Billy Wickham, but at half time was moved to centerfield, a position I held for many years. A few weeks after the county final, I played for the club in a tournament against Eire Óg of Kilkenny, and it was from this game that I was picked to play for the county. Needless to say, I was delighted and very surprised.

My first problem now was my boots and shorts. Were they good enough to take to Croke Park? I don't think the present generation understands what it was like back then, how difficult it was for a family of six or eight to have money to buy anything other than the bare necessities of life. It was not long after World War II, and clothing and footwear of good quality were both expensive and hard to get. The studs in my boots were made of leather, but they had become very short and worn. So I got a piece of soleing leather and put two strips across the sole of each boot, and one across the heel; then, into these I drove a row of boot nails. This made the boots a bit heavy, but at least I would stay on my feet in

Croke Park.

The next difficulty was my shorts, (we called them 'nicks' back then), so, after having a word with my mother, who held the purse in our home, I got on my bike and headed for Enniscorthy. As there was only one shop in the town that sold sports goods, I didn't have much choice. I was shown two pairs of shorts, one cost the equivalent of 42 cents, the other 25 cents. After feeling the cloth in each, I decided the cheaper one was good enough; it felt a bit hard, but I thought, given a wash it would be fine. When my mother saw it, she said, "That thing is full of starch", and she gave it a shake. A lot of dust flew from it, so she put it into a basin of hot water to remove the starch. When it was washed and dried, you could see through the damn thing, so now I really did have a problem. Very few men wore underpants in those days, so you can understand my fear - if the weather stayed dry I could get away with it, but what if we had heavy rain? Anyway, I brought my old pair, too, just in case.

My hurl was pretty OK. It was made by a man called Kinsella from Oylegate, and had the old-style long boss - I think he was the last man to make that old style stick. I put a few extra nails into the band on it, just in case it needed them. My gear then consisted of one hurl, one pair of boots, one pair of socks, two pairs of shorts and two garters. There were no fancy sports bags then. You folded the shorts and socks, put them between the boots, wrapped the bootlaces around the bundle and tied them tightly. Then you shoved the handle of the hurl between the boots. If properly done, the bundle would never slip over the boss, so your gear was safe.

The arrangements for the journey to Croke Park were that Bobby Rackard would bring the family car and I would go with him. Billy Rackard was playing his first game on this occasion, too, so he was travelling with us. Bobby's brother John and a young lad by the name of Coogan, who worked in

Rackard's, made it five in a small car. John Rackard was six feet four inches tall, so he sat in the front with Bobby, and we smaller lads sat in the back. We hadn't gone very far when I was feeling sick, very sick. For years this was a problem for me going to games. I would feel really sick, but never had to stop the car. Bobby was never known to spare a car, and that didn't help. We got to Dublin in good time, had a cup of tea, and after about an hour I felt fine. There were no nerves or worries. We were going to do our best, and that was it.

The Wexford team which played against Dublin on that day in November '49 was:

Art Foley

Mick O'Hanlon	Martin Byrne	Billy Rackard
Sam 'Wilkie' Thorpe	Bobby Rackard	Billy Stamp

Martin Codd   Jim Morrissey

Des O'Neill	Padge Kehoe	Dominic Hearn
Sean Flood	Bobby Donovan	Tim Flood

When we went into the dressing room in Croke Park, I had a look around and there were only ten or eleven people there that I had seen before. I didn't know any selector or County Board official. When everyone was togged out, we were told our positions on the field, but nothing more. As we left the dressing room to walk down the concrete passage to the pitch, I noticed my boots were making a much louder sound than those of the other lads. Some old fellow said, "By God, you're well shod, young fella!" For the first time, I wondered if I was taking on more than I could handle. I took a little run up the four or five steps that led onto the pitch. When my feet hit the grass I gave a few swings of the hurl, and I felt at ease. The sod was like a carpet - if you could hurl at all, you could do it here. By contrast, the field back home was on a bit of a brow, with some rushes growing on the lower sideline.

There was no such thing as the players racing from the dressing room then; I don't think we even had a ball for a puck around. When I got out on the park and looked around the place, it was frightening. The stands were huge, and so high! The crowd was small, mostly Dubs standing on Hill 16 and shouting in an accent that was hard to understand. We had only a handful of supporters there, mostly Wexford people working or living in the city, I'd say.

Just before the teams lined up for the start of the game, Jim Morrissey came to me and said, "Which side do you want to play on?" I hadn't even thought about it, so I said, "I don't mind". Those were the first words we ever spoke to each other. Jim said, "Des Dillon is playing on the right and he's pretty good, I'll take him, and you go on the other fella."

Before the ball was thrown in, Tim Flood said to me, "This may be the one time we'll play in this place, so we'll show them." I hadn't thought of it in that way, so I told myself, "It won't be for the want of trying. I'll chase everything that's stirring", and that's what I did. Many years later, Dr. Bob Bowe, who was a great supporter of Wexford, said to me, "I remember the first time you played in Croke Park; you were like a hare that was let out of a bag".

I don't remember a lot about the game itself. We were beaten by two points, but I was happy with the way I'd played. What I do remember were the surroundings and in particular the pitch: it was so easy to lift the ball, or to hit it on the ground. It was a great place to hurl, and I couldn't wait to get back there again.

As winter was now settling in, there would be no more games until the spring. These players would not be together again for two or three months. The only one I would meet, almost every day for a while, was Tim Flood. Tim's father owned a farm and had thrashing sets for hire. Tim worked with one set, thrashing the corn for the farmers around the area. A thrashing required a large number of workers, and, being a farmer's son, I would be sent to help the neighbouring farmers. Tim and I would, therefore, meet almost every day for a few weeks. After dinner at the thrashing, there would be a break for the hard-working men to have a smoke and a rest, but not for Tim Flood. He would challenge someone to a feat of strength or skill, and soon the place would be something like a circus. The contest could be lifting weights or a sack of barley; it could be climbing the pillars of the hayshed, or crossing the roof of the shed, swinging from the roof supports.

There were many more tricks he'd get up to, but Tim's favourite was to get someone to sit on the ground opposite him and to put the soles of their feet against his. Each would then grasp the handle of a pitchfork and pull until one of them was lifted off the ground. I never saw Tim beaten at this. Looking back on it now, I suppose that was how we got the upper-body strength and the strength in our hands, that is so important for hurlers. We had never heard of a gym then.

We also talked a lot about hurling. Tim, whose mother came from Limerick, once told me about being brought to a Munster final and seeing Mick Mackey and the great Limerick team. Another thing which gave great inspiration to us young lads was Michael O'Hehir's radio-commentary on games. The first one I heard was the hurling final of 1940 between Limerick and Kilkenny, when I was eleven years old. I can still remember the names of the players. There was no radio in our house at the time, so my father let me go across the two fields to Martin Murphy's house to hear the game. Martin Murphy was the father of Ferdy Murphy, the well-known horse trainer, now living in England. And race-goers might also be interested to know that if I had crossed three more fields, I'd have come to the home of Aidan O'Brien, the even better-known horse trainer. I'm rambling a bit now, but what I'm trying to point out is what life was like for young lads in the '40s, and the things that started the hurling dream.

1950

The team selectors appointed for 1950 were Eamonn Cullen, Nick Bowe, Jim Walsh, Tom Kehoe, and Mikie Redmond. An important development that year also was the appointment of Sean Brown as Chairman of the GAA County Board. This proved a wise choice as Sean was a great organiser, and held the position all through the '50s.

Wexford's first game in the New Year was against Laois in the National League. It was played in Bellefield, Enniscorthy, on 26 February. As Laois were Leinster champions, there was quite an amount of interest among the faithful Wexford hurling followers and a good number turned up for the match. The weather was poor on the day and the ground very soft, so the standard of hurling was not good. We played a draw with the Leinster champions, so our followers were happy. Still, there were those who said, wait until you meet the strong counties, then we'll see the men sorted from the boys.

The Wexford team that day was,

Art Foley

Mick O'Hanlon	Martin Byrne	Billy Rackard
Sam Thorpe	Bobby Rackard	Billy Stamp

Martin Codd   Jim Morrissey

Dominic Hearne	Padge Kehoe	Tim Russell
Tim Flood	Tim Lenihan	Nickey Rackard

There would still be lots of difficulties in trying to build a good hurling team in those early years as most people in the county thought the future was in football. Nickey Rackard, Padge Kehoe, Sam Thorpe, Des O'Neill and Mick Hanlon were all proven inter-county footballers, and would be expected to turn out for the football team if there was a clash of dates.

What was really driving interest in hurling forward in the

county at this time was the great rivalry between the three neighbouring clubs, St Aidan's of Enniscorthy, Rathnure and Cloughbawn. Boys from both Rathnure and Cloughbawn had played minor with Enniscorthy when there were no underage teams in their own clubs. Cloughbawn boys had also won minor hurling medals with Rathnure, so, when these lads progressed to playing senior grade for their own clubs, you could cut the rivalry with a knife; it really brought the best out of everyone. The rest of the county took sides too, with the result it brought great crowds to matches and a whole new interest to hurling. There was never a bad tempered or dirty game between these teams, and the rivalry they had at club level was never brought to the county team.

Wexford's first games in the 1950 championship were against Meath and Offaly. Neither of these counties would be considered strong, so it was no surprise when both games were won easily. Still, they gave the selectors a chance to sort players out and get the best team available on the pitch for the bigger games to come.

The provincial champions, Laois, were the opposition in the Leinster semi-final, and the match was fixed for Kilkenny. As we had already played a draw with them in the League, there was an increased amount of interest in the game throughout the county. The team chosen was:

Art Foley

Billy Rackard	Martin Byrne	Mick O'Hanlon
Sam Thorpe	Bobby Rackard	Ned Wheeler

Padge Kehoe   Jim Morrissey

Dominic Hearn	Nickey Rackard	Tim Russell
Bobby Donovan	Jim Quinn	Tim Flood

It's worth noting that the name Ned Wheeler appeared here on the team sheet for the first time. Wheeler was just eighteen years old and had been outstanding on the county minor team. Another outstanding minor that year was Jim

English, who had played at centre forward, but his day with the seniors was yet to come.

From the point of view of neutral spectators, the game was a disappointment, with Wexford scoring a bag of goals and winning, 7-02 to 1-06. But the win gave our supporters hope for better things to come. They now looked forward keenly to the Leinster final against Kilkenny.

For some reason, this game was fixed for Nowlan Park in Kilkenny, instead of at a neutral venue. This left Wexford at a disadvantage. We were nervous and unsure of what way things would go. However, looking back at this Leinster final against Kilkenny, I think it was the game which, more than anything else, changed Wexford from a football to a hurling county.

The team picked for the big day was:

Art Foley

| Billy Rackard | Martin Byrne | Mick O'Hanlon |
| Martin Flood | Bobby Rackard | Sam Thorpe |

Martin Codd   Jim Morrissey

| Dominic Hearne | Padge Kehoe | Tim Russell |
| Bobby Donovan | Nickey Rackard | Tim Flood. |

I had been living in London for four months at this time. Not having any contacts in London when I arrived there, my involvement in the game of hurling was a bit chaotic. On the advice of a workmate, I went to the Wormwood Scrubs Park one Sunday where, he said, most teams practised. Wormwood Scrubs was a huge public park and people went there to play all kinds of games. I borrowed a hurl from the first group of lads I saw practising and got involved in their game. After a short while I was approached by a man who asked me where I came from. When I told him I had been playing for Wexford he got very interested and he asked me if I would play for his club the following Sunday. Being a bit naïve, I said "Sure, I'd be delighted". So it was arranged that I would meet up with a few of the players from this team in a pub at twelve o'clock the following Sunday.

After some difficulty finding this pub and being half an hour late, I discovered that the game was not until 3 o'clock and we would be in the pub until 2 o'clock. To this day I believe destiny led me to that pub and what took place there fifty five years ago. The first question I was asked by one of the lads was "What are you drinking?" I said, "I don't drink". "Well you're going to drink now", was the answer. I said "No, thank you". A glass of beer was bought and put in front of me and the conversation turned to hurling. After a while one of the lads said to me "Are you not going to drink that pint after I buying it for you?" Again I said, "I don't drink", and with that, he grabbed the Pioneer Total Abstinence badge that I was wearing and pulled it from my jacket. "Now," he said, "you can drink". Whatever kind of effect his actions had on me, I swore to myself that I would never drink alcoholic drinks, and I never have.

After these three lads had put away at least five pints each we went on to play the match. I felt trapped and didn't want to play in a game with fellows who were full of beer. But I decided to go through with it even though I didn't know the name of the club I was going to play for, or who the opposition was. I discovered later I was playing for St Mary's, but to this day I don't know who we I played against. Just before the ball was thrown in to start the game, I was told by the official who had asked me to play for his team that if I was asked my name I was to say Jimmy McInerney. Right away I knew there was something illegal going on here, but I could see no way out. Being very shy and not knowing anyone at the game, I went ahead and played the match.

When the game was over I was approached by a man who asked me if I would play for London a few weeks later in Oxford against Oxfordshire. I said sure, why not. He then told me I had been playing on a man by the name of Power who had played for Munster and that I had done very well. He told me what the travel arrangements would be for the game in Oxford and, as we parted, he said, "I'll see you on Sunday week, Jimmy". Although I was now getting a bit confused, I bought a new set of boots, socks and shorts and went to the 'Scrubs Park the following Sunday again. I had no hurl so, with my boots under my arm, I kept strolling around the place. There were soccer and cricket matches going on, but I could see no hurling.

Eventually a fellow came up to me and said, "Are you looking for a game, Paddy?" Being the idiot I was at that time, I said, "Should I know you?" "I don't think so", he said, "I was just looking for an extra player or two to make a second team so we can have a bit of fun and a bit of exercise". I thought to myself: sure a bit of football will keep me fit, so I went with him to the playing pitch where about twenty men were togged out and ready to go. In all my life I have never seen such a collection in togs. They looked like middle aged business men and were very big and overweight. It was only when I saw the shape of the ball I realised I was going to play rugby. I had never seen a rugby match and knew nothing about the rules of the game, but the man who recruited me soon put that right. "You play full back, Paddy", he said, "and every time the ball comes into your territory just collect it and kick for touch". The game was over in half an hour and the most entertaining part for me was the scrums. I never heard such grunts and groans and farts. The latter were quite musical, something like a child trying to play a bassoon. Once, in good Gaelic style, I went high for a ball and sent a good long clearance down the field. I heard my tutor shout, "Well done, Paddy, what a lovely fetch!" To tell the truth, these men were very nice and thanked me for my contribution to their game.

I went to Oxford the following Sunday and played hurling for London. The only other game I remember playing was a football match I played for Round Towers. Most of this team were Kildare men and I was put in touch with them by my workmate who seemed to know everything about the GAA in London. The man I was marking that day told me he was Fr Kevin Connolly - the great Louth footballer. I also knew him as the Irish National Sprint Champion.

It was now mid-June, and Wexford had qualified to meet Kilkenny in the Leinster Hurling Final. I decided that I would go back home and perhaps get my place on the Wexford team again. But I could have a problem. Surely I had made myself illegal by playing in London. My workmate was able to give me the date of the June meeting of the London GAA County Board. So I decided I would go to this meeting and find out what my position was. The chairman of the County Board at that time was a man by the name of Mullarkey. There were very few people at the meeting and not much business to be done. I told the meeting I had been in London for less than four months and that I had played four games, but didn't know if those games were in official competitions or not. I said I didn't think I was registered with any club, as no one had ever called me by my proper name. I said I was going home in a few days and that I would not be back. The chairman looked at me over his spectacles for a few seconds and seemed very puzzled. He turned to the man sitting on his left and they had a few words. He then said something to the man on his right, who just nodded in agreement. Then he looked at me again and said "You are definitely going home?" I said, "Yes, sir, in a few days time". "In that case", he said, "forget you were ever here". I thanked him and left the meeting. Ten days before the Leinster final, I was back home and was called into the team again because a couple of the players had injuries. The only hurling I had done in the four months away was to play the three games in London, but at twenty years of age I had no problems with fitness. I had played a few League matches for the county, but no championship match before going to England. My big worry and I know it worried other members of the team as well, was the quality of the opposition.

More than half of this Wexford team were playing inter-county hurling for less than a year. There were no coaches or sports psychologists back then, so we just got on with it as best we could. What usually took place when the players were togged out and ready to go out on the pitch was that the County Chairman, Sean Browne, would call the team together and say a few things like, "Get out there now, lads, and give it your best, move the ball fast on the ground and don't start poking and prodding at it. Nickey and Padge will take the close-in frees, and Bobby will take the seventies. Don't say anything to the ref, and if you're asked to lie down, do so quickly and come off."

In those days the rules of the game required that a player must be injured before he could be replaced. You might think you were having a pretty good game when, suddenly, you'd hear one of the mentors shouting at you "Lie down!" You'd then wait until the play came into your area again and try to get into some kind of tackle. Down you'd go, holding your knee or an ankle, to wait for the fellow with the bottle of water to arrive. Following a brief consultation, he'd lift you up and help you limp to the sideline, watched by a cynical and unsympathetic crowd.

I saw a player one day, in a club match, getting the call to lie down as he was getting involved in a bit of a ruck in the goalmouth. He dropped down flat where he was and, as it was a wet day, he went down in a big lough of water; being a good actor, he stayed put until the man with the bottle arrived and rescued him. It wasn't a nice thing to be told to lie down; it always reminded me of a farmer with a sheepdog - when the dog took a wrong turn the farmer would shout, "Lie down, Shep!"

The Kilkenny team consisted of men we had all read about in the newspapers, and heard about on the radio, but some of us had never seen them play: I had seen their photos in the paper so often, I'd have no problem recognising most of them. For two or three nights before the game I woke up in a sweat when, in my dreams, I'd see the faces of men like Raymie Dowling, Diamond Hayden, Mark Marnell, Paddy Buggy, Willie Walsh, Shem Downey, Jack Gargan, Jimmie Langton, Jimmie Heffernan, Dan Kennedy, Liam Reidy, all members of the Kilkenny team. I prayed, not that we'd win but that we wouldn't be humiliated.

Close to forty thousand people arrived in Kilkenny for the game, creating huge problems for the officials in charge. There were not enough stewards to control the crowd, more than half were from Wexford. It would have been the first time big numbers came from the football strongholds in the south and the north of the county, and all expected to have a good view of the action. There were very few buses in the county at the time to bring people to the games, and cars were few and far between, so people got there as best they could. Some rode their bicycles, and some even went the day before in their pony and traps. Lorries were not plentiful either, but every coal lorry or scut lorry that had four wheels was on the road. People put stools and chairs in the lorries and sat for two or three hours bumping along on poor springs over the pot holes and humps in the roads. Many of them told me that they couldn't sit down for a week after a match.

When we got to Kilkenny and saw the masses of people on the streets, it was frightening, they seemed to be going in all directions. Many of the Wexford supporters, I'd say, had never been in a crowd like this before. Because there weren't enough turnstiles to allow such a crowd of spectators quick access to the park, people were being crushed against the walls. Our struggle to reach the dressing rooms took our minds off the game for a while.

Inside the park, there were people all along the sidelines, at the back of both goals, and on the walls surrounding the park. This was by far the biggest attendance we had yet seen. Before ever the match started, the spectators seemed very excited and agitated as they pushed and shoved to get a view. A couple of small angry Rathnure men afterwards told me that the only time they saw the ball was when it went high in the air. This was also the first time a game involving this Wexford team was broadcast on radio. Michael O'Hehir was doing the commentary, and by the end of the match he had to leave his commentary box; the spectators were impeding his view and he had to come down to the sideline so he could follow the play.

Of the Wexford team, only Nickey Rackard and "Wilkie" Thorpe would have been involved in a situation with any resemblance to this; having played with the county football team, they would have had some experience of crowds. There was a strange feeling in the dressing room that day as we togged out. It was quiet, with everyone speaking in hushed tones - the feeling may have been that we were going out to be massacred.

When the time came to go out on the field, Sean Browne called us together and said his few words, and then asked Nickey Rackard to speak. Throughout the career of this team, when things were tough and our backs were to the wall, Nickey was the man who did the talking. When Nickey stepped out to the middle of the floor with his hurl in his hand, most of us were sitting around looking somewhat like the proverbial sheep waiting to be led to the slaughterhouse.

"Look here, lads," Nickey began, "we've been forced to play

these fellas in their own backyard, and the Dublin press have been saying all week that we're going to be taught a lesson here. But I don't think so." He raised his voice. "Stand up, lads, stand up so I can see you". Every one of us jumped to our feet. There was fire in Nickey's eyes as he slowly turned, looking each player in the eye. "Is there one man here who thinks we are going to be beaten today? If there is, let him put his clothes back on, and go home now. These Kilkenny lads have All-Ireland medals in their pockets, and what have we? Nothing! Not even a Leinster medal, but today we can change that; they are only men like any of us. For years we have dreamt about a day like this; don't let it pass by without a fight. Wexford men have never been afraid of a fight, and there are twenty thousand of them out there now waiting to roar their heads off for us fellas. They're here from every corner of the county, and we're not going to let them down. Get out there, and do Wexford proud!"

Nine of the team were new to this level of competition, and it was evident in our faces as we left the dressing room. With people everywhere, it was a struggle to get out onto the pitch.

If there was a parade of the teams before the game, I don't remember it; but I do remember the "throw in" and the roar of the crowd. Wexford got off to a flying start with two points from Padge Kehoe and one from Jim Morrissey. Kilkenny drew level with a goal. Nickey Rackard was pulled down as he was going through for a score. Awarded a 21 yards free, he scored a goal. Over the next several years these scores became known as "Rackard Specials".

Nickey had developed a unique way of taking these frees for which the ball was placed 21 yards from the goal line. He went three or four paces back from the ball, then, taking a few quick strides, he raised the ball with his hurl, tossing it forward and, continuing his run, he struck it with all his might. Even with several players lining the goal, seldom were these shots saved. This day in Kilkenny he almost tore the net from the goalposts as the Wexford crowd went wild, and the scores were level for a second time.

Minutes later Nickey got possession again, rounded his man and, once more, the net shook. This was the first time Wexford supporters had experienced this kind of stuff, and they were showing it along the sideline - the pitch seemed to be getting narrower. Kilkenny scored a point and Jim Morrissey did likewise for Wexford. Kilkenny had the last score of the first half, a point. This left the score at halftime, Wexford 2-06, Kilkenny 2-04.

We were very happy with our situation as we headed for the dressing room. Again, we had some difficulty reaching our destination, but, when we got there, there was a cup of tea waiting for us. It was the first time a luxury of this kind was offered to us, and I thought it a good idea.

The whole atmosphere in the dressing-room was different now. Everyone was talking and encouraging each other. As we were going out for the second half, Nickey said, "Keep it up, lads, and we'll bring something home from here tonight." There was a lot of confusion and noise when we got back on the pitch, with stewards and officials trying to move people back from the sidelines. There was a breeze and we would feel it against us in the second half.

It was immediately evident that the Kilkenny players had been given a serious lecture on what needed to be done. Their marking was much tighter, and two or three of our lads were getting special attention. Twice Bobby Rackard was badly tackled as he was clearing the ball, not by his immediate opponent, but by one who came in from the side and lashed down on his hands. In over twenty years of playing hurling and football with Bobby, I never saw him hit a dirty stroke. But, after this game, it was remarked how a certain Kilkenny player faded out of the game completely, with a badly swollen face and one eye almost closed, as if he had been hit in the eye with the ball. Bobby spoke up and said, "No, he ran into a short left hook". You didn't question Bobby about how that happened.

With the help of the wind, Kilkenny went looking for scores. Under a lot of pressure, Artie Foley parried a ball and, as I saw it, he cleared it out the field, but I'll quote Billy Rackard's version of events. To this day, Billy says he was on the end line, close to the goal. Artie blocked the ball, it spun on the goal-line, and he lashed it to safety. One umpire, who was behind Artie, shouted "Goal!", and went to wave the green flag. But the umpire who was facing Artie, and who would have had the best view of the ball, shook his head and shouted, "No!" The referee, who was forty yards out the field where he could not see what really happened, ran a bit towards the goal, then stopped, signalled the green flag to be raised, wrote down the score and went on with the game. I have no recollection of the ball being pucked out.

This goal gave Kilkenny a one point lead, but Wexford came back and had points from Tim Russell, Tim Flood, Nickey Rackard and Padge Kehoe. It was in this game I first realised the value of being good at striking the ball overhead. Jim Morrissey and myself had given an exhibition of this skill in the first half when the puck out from our goal reached mid-field. But now, with the wind getting much stronger, the puck out was dropping short. I still remember how, in frustration at not being able to win the puck out, I moved back to within forty yards of our goal so that the ball could be hit to me. I was now again able to strike it overhead and send it downfield, only to see my marker, Willie Walsh, who stayed in his midfield position, collect it and send it back over the bar. Kilkenny scored five unanswered points at this stage of the game, which gave them a two points lead.

With time running out, we got the ball down to the

forwards, and Nickey sent over a point. Then Kilkenny got a point, which I and many people at the back of the goal thought was a wide. From the short puck out, Kilkenny got what was to be their final score.

Knowing that time was now almost up, the crowd were well in on the pitch, but Wexford made one final burst. There was confusion everywhere as one of the Wexford players was dragged to the ground about thirty yards from the Kilkenny goal. Because only a goal would do to even the scores, Nickey went for one of his specials. He was too far from the goal and the shot was blocked. The ball was cleared out the field, where Tim Russell collected it and headed for the goal.

There are different versions of what happened next, but, as I remember it, Tim received a heavy tackle and was fouled. Thinking he had a free, he dropped the ball for Nickey to take another of his "specials", it being well within his range. But the referee picked up the ball and, without blowing his whistle, threw it in between the two players standing nearest him, he then turned and ran towards the dressing rooms. Paddy Grace, the Kilkenny County Secretary, met him half way, put his arm around him to protect him, and they disappeared into the crowd.

To say there was chaos now, would be an understatement. The players and spectators alike were totally confused and a free-for-all took place. I was one of the first to reach our dressing room, and it seemed an age before the last man arrived. There were no reports of anyone being killed, but I believe some rough stuff went on out there. The trouble at the game was later discussed at Central Council, but no action was taken.

Looking back now, after all the years, on that game in Kilkenny, I can see more clearly than ever what the events of that one day did for hurling in Wexford. When Nickey Rackard said to the team at half time, "Keep it up, lads, and we'll bring something home from here tonight", his words were so true. We may not have brought home victory, but we brought a belief in ourselves and a dream that was shared by every Wexford man and woman who was in Nowlan Park that day. Another thing that started that day was the strange relationship that exists between Kilkenny and the Wexford supporters. Before 1950, Wexford people were good supporters of Kilkenny, but today they will only support Kilkenny if they are playing Cork or, perhaps, Tipperary. Since 1950, Kilkenny folk are always afraid Wexford might beat them, a result which is always an embarrassment for them.

Something else which started that day also is the great camaraderie which exists in Wexford teams, and the wonderful support they get from the whole county. For the emerging hurling supporter, and there were many of them now, prospects for the future were looking good; there was a lot of work still to be done, only time and patience would bring success, but a flame had been lit and the rest of the country was beginning to take notice.

After the Leinster final the team was invited to play a number of exhibitions for charitable purposes, and in August we set off to play a London selection in London. These games were not taken very seriously, but it gave the players and their mentors the opportunity to get to know each other. Half of the team did not take a drink, and the other half had no money to buy any, but we always had a great time on these occasions.

In the fall of 1950, Wexford was, for the first time, invited to play in the Oireachtas Cup competition. Each year four of the best hurling teams in the country were invited to play for this cup, so we considered it an honour for Wexford to take part. It was a great experience to play against the top teams, and Wexford made good use of this competition when given the opportunity over the next several years. There would be big crowds at these games, with the added experience of playing in Croke Park. For one reason or another, every game we played in was now getting great coverage in the daily press, and many of the neutrals among attendances were beginning to support us.

The four teams competing for the cup in 1950 were Cork, Wexford, Kilkenny and Galway; Tipperary, who were All-Ireland champions, withdrew as they were making a trip to America. A huge crowd turned out in Wexford Park for our semi-final against Cork. After a good performance, we won by 4-10 to 3-02. Paddy Kehoe, of Gusserane, re-appeared on the hurling team for this game. He was one of the most skilful hurlers the county ever produced, but he was an even better footballer. However, like a few more of the dual players on the hurling panel, it was make-your-mind-up-time for Paddy.

Galway beat Kilkenny in the other semi-final in Nowlan Park, and the final between Galway and Wexford was fixed for Croke Park in mid-October. Since neither team had won any competition for over twenty-five years and they knew very little about each other's style of play, it was going to be a novel occasion. The press warned that, as both teams played robust hurling, the game would need a strict referee, but after the game they had a different story.

It was described as the game of the year, between two brilliant teams. There were hard knocks given and taken by two great sets of sporting players. The final score was, Galway 2-09, Wexford 2-06. We were beaten, but were gaining more and more admirers in the press and among the followers of hurling. One of the things I'll never forget about this game was the free-taking of Galway's Josie Gallagher; any free within thirty yards of the goal, he just cut it off the ground and over the bar. I never saw it done before or since.

We now turned our attention to the National League. The

A recent photo of Kitty and myself with our nine children. Back from left: Pat, Martin, Austin, Kevin, John, Mike. The three girls are, from left: Agnes, Mary and Jacqueline.

Nickey Rackard's daughters Marion (left) and Bernadette holding the picture of their father while Billie holds the picture of Bobby. On the right is John Rackard. The pictures are replicas of those used for the Millennium Stamp Collection which were presented to Rathnure GAA Club by An Post.

Nick O'Donnell's daughter Ann with the glass replica of the McCarthy Cup which was presented to all former Captains of All-Ireland winning teams by the GAA. Nick 'O was Captain in 1955 and 1960 when Wexford won. Also included is the framed photo presented to Nick's family by An Post when he was selected full-back on the Team of the Millennium.

With my son Mike and grandson Paul. The only father, son and grandson to win Oireachtas medals - correct me if I'm wrong.

Jim English with the glass replica of the McCarthy Cup which
the GAA presented to all captains of All-Ireland winning teams.
Jim was captain in 1956. Also in the photo are some more of
Jim's trophies.

The old school in Rathnure where the Rackards and I went to
school. It is now renovated and preserved for posterity.

From left, Ted Bolger, Padge Kehoe and Tom Dixon, three great Enniscorthy men who, between them, won 21 County Championship medals with the St. Aidan's Club.

Will we ever again see the likes of Rackard and Ring? seen here with P.A. (Weeshie) Murphy of Cork on the left.

Waiting for the parade to start in the Polo Grounds, New York. Jim (Tough) Barry, (encircled in yellow), of Cork in his red jumper is behind the drummer with the white Aran sweater.

Paddy Kehoe ready for action in the Polo Grounds, New York. Sean Flood, who played a number of games for Wexford in the early '50s, is on his right.

reward for winning it in 1950-51 included a trip to New York
for a two-week holiday. A trip of this kind in 1951 would be
like going to the moon today. When we set out for Thurles to
play Tipperary in our first game in the competition, the trip
to America was far from our minds. Tipp who were All-
Ireland champions in '49 and '50, were the current League
champions; they had not been beaten for two and a half years
and would be playing on their home ground, so our concern
was understandable. On top of that, for our first time, we
were going to play in Thurles, the birthplace of the GAA,
where, we were told, the ball would travel faster on the sod
than anywhere else in the land. When we arrived at Hayes's
hotel in the town that day, we were reminded by some of the
Tipperary officials that it was here the first meeting of the
GAA was held, that here the whole thing was founded.

The Wexford football team was playing Waterford on the
same day and there was a lot of speculation as to which team
the dual players would play for. There was a trip to New York
for the winners of the football League that year also. One of
the papers had been running a poll to find out who its
readers thought were the top teams in the country. Wexford
footballers were voted into fourth place, with the hurlers at
number five. Waterford would not have been considered a
threat to the football team, so we were delighted to see that
Nickey Rackard and Paddy Kehoe were coming to Thurles -
the respective selectors may have met and reached a
compromise.

For the hurling team, this game was another milestone on
the road to greatness. We knew we were facing one of the
greatest teams of all time. A year earlier we would have been
afraid of being humiliated, but now all that was changing.
Although the Tipp team were big and physical, we had no
fear of that side of their game. Whatever this Wexford team
was short of, it was never going to be courage. We feared no

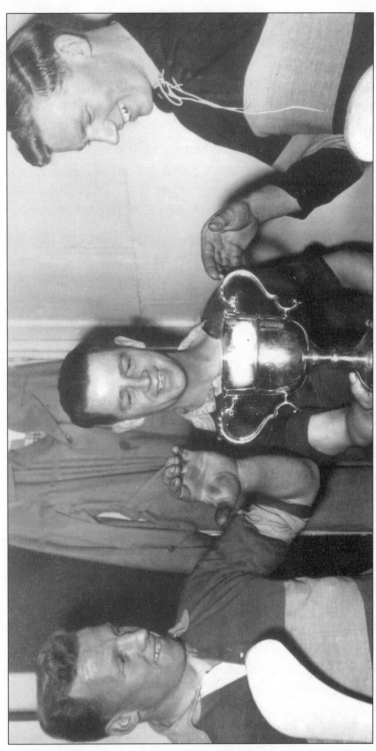

Picture taken in Sam Melbourne Museum in Thurles prior to the League Final of 1956. Tommy Doyle in the centre with Mickey Byrne, Tipp, on his right and Jim English on his left.

one physically, and could take care of ourselves without stooping to foul means. Though it is now over fifty years since we played this game, it is one that I still remember very well. Despite the footballers playing much nearer home, in Waterford, the bigger contingent of supporters travelled to Thurles.

The team that faced Tipperary that day was:

Art Foley

Mikie Walsh   Martin Byrne   Mick O'Hanlon

Billy Rackard   Bobby Rackard   Ned Wheeler

Jim Morrissey   Martin Codd

Padge Kehoe   Paddy Kehoe   Tim Russell

Dom Hearne   Nickey Rackard   Tim Flood.

Of all the great players on the Tipperary team, the one I most wanted to see was Tommy Doyle. Tommy had won an All-Ireland medal as far back as 1937, when I was only eight years old, and he was still going strong. His greatest achievement was in 1949 when, in 150 minutes of championship hurling, he held Christy Ring scoreless. Cork and Tipperary played a draw in the Munster championship, a replay and thirty minutes extra time, and although he was over thirty years of age, Tommy was still there at the finish. He was a wonderful ground hurler, who seldom fouled. He was a great hero of Tim Flood's, and this day he was going to be marking Tim. In the car on our way to Thurles, we had been discussing all this, and wondering how Jim Morrissey and I would fare on Phil Shanahan and Seamus Bannon at centerfield. We came to the conclusion that we would at least hold our own, which gives an idea of how our confidence was growing.

Jim Morrissey never said much during a game, but when something needed to be said, he would walk past you and, without moving his lips, would mutter to you under his breath. Just before the throw-in, Jim muttered to me, "You go after Bannon, you'll keep up with him better than I would, and I'll go on this other big so-and-so". A great expression of Jim's was, "You look after your own patch and let everyone else do the same".

The Wexford team was really fired-up for this game and started at a ferocious pace. I don't think the Tipperary followers liked this, they had come there to see their team give an exhibition, so they soon became very vocal. The Tipperary players did not believe in sidesteps or going around opponents, that would be a sign of weakness. No! They just came straight at you. These tactics suited the big Wexford men, and right from the start we had a fierce battle of strength and skill. Next day some of the pressmen described Wexford as playing with "controlled aggression". We hadn't yet even thought about tactics or a game plan; but we just knew there was no place for the jibber or the messer.

They say, to have excitement in a game you need goals; well, this match had fourteen, some of them brilliant scores. As Jim Morrissey would say, he and I were looking after our own patch, and doing quite well, too. I was playing on Seamus Bannon, a real speed merchant; but speed is of little use while the ball is in the air, you must wait till it hits the ground. From the beginning, I was able to get under every puck-out that came my way and strike it on overhead to our forwards, until just before half time, when Bannon changed his tactics. He began to stand well behind me; then he would come racing in at the last second, and with his hurl in one hand, jump up to flick the ball away, leaving me pulling on fresh air and looking rather silly.

When we went into the dressing room at half time, Patsy Boggan took me to one side and said, "That fella is after beating you to the last two or three puck-outs; you'll have to try something different or he is going to get the better of you. The next ball that's dropping down, get under it as if you're to hit it on your right; then, at the last second, take a step across and hit it on your left". I always took heed of men like Patsy; I knew they were there to help us.

We were two goals down at half time, even though we had played quite well. In the dressing room everyone seemed to be talking at the same time, encouraging each other and rearing to get on with the game. As we went back out on the pitch, I was trying to remember all Patsy Boggan had told me, and going over it in my head. The pitch seemed bigger and better than anywhere else I had played, and there was a lot of ground to cover at centre field. I liked the open spaces and felt confident I would do well in the second half.

Anyway, the first puck-out that came my way I got under it, but stepped across at the last second to hit it on my left; before I swung at all, Bannon landed on my back and I had a free. The next dropping ball I got under, the same thing happened, and again I had my free. I didn't have any more trouble that day, thanks to Patsy Boggan.

In the second half the backs were outstanding, with Bobby Rackard surpassing anything we had seen from him before. We got completely on top at centerfield and, with a good supply of the ball, the forwards went to town. At fourteen stone weight Paddy Kehoe was like a tank. With speed and skill, he tore the backs to ribbons. Nickey Rackard was inspiring. He scored two goals from play, and one of his "specials".

At most venues where games were played in the 1950s, there were no scoreboards, but in Thurles there was a nice big one, with big white numbers which, that evening read, Wexford 8-08, Tipperary 6-06. As we left the pitch, I looked back at it several times. 'Twas unbelievable! This game raised our team to a new level. Sports journalists around the country realised they had something new, different and exciting to write about.

Nothing gives a young player more confidence in his own ability than to play on a great player and hold his own. That day in Thurles we played on and beat the best in the game. Going home that evening, our confidence was sky high, but we still had a lot to learn, as time would tell. Many times we would be awakened from our dream. The following Sunday we played Dublin in the League in Wexford Park and won, 6-07 to 5-06.

That was our final game for 1950, and what a year it had been! In the space of twelve months we had come from being "no hopers" to being serious contenders for major honours. If the Leinster final against Kilkenny had been played in Croke Park, we felt we would have won it, and who knows what would have happened after that.

1951

It would be three months before our next League match, so, both players and supporters would have plenty of time to contemplate the future. There would be no organised winter training for the team, but each one of us had his own routine for keeping fit. I remember mine as if it was yesterday. Almost every day after dinner I would spend fifteen or twenty minutes hurling in the yard with a rubber ball. This yard measured about fifteen yards by thirty. On one side was a lofted cowshed, on the other a garden wall about five feet high; at one end was a lofted stable and at the other a piggery with an eight foot wall. I would hit the ball hard so that it would glance off the ground about three yards from the wall; it would then strike the wall in an upward direction and come back to me high in the air. Now I could hit it, right or left, high as I could reach, against either wall, and then lash it about until I got in a position to begin the whole routine again. Seldom do you see players even attempt to strike the ball overhead in today's game. It's a lovely skill, and can be very effective.

At this time in rural Ireland, where most of the team were living, things were very primitive by present day standards. There was no electricity, no water on tap and very few tractors. Most farm work was done with horses, and all digging and excavation was done with a pick and shovel. Sacks of corn and fertiliser, etc., weighing sixteen stone or more, were manhandled. The game of hurling, too, was more physical then.

Not knowing what training the other lads were doing, I thought to myself, I'll get tough and skilful over the winter months, and then I can't go wrong. I was twenty years old, six feet two inches tall, and weighing just thirteen stone. I was married and my wife Kitty was expecting our first child in

March. This meant that my first priority was my family, with hurling a close second.

Emigration was rampant, with most young people going to England. Out of my class in Rathnure school, nine of the fourteen had already gone. There were no jobs here. One way of making a few pounds in the winter months, was by catching rabbits and wood pigeons and selling them for the English market. Since the war years meat and some other commodities were still rationed in Great Britain. I think the rabbits were sold on the black market and that made them expensive, which was good for the Irish side of the business. Rabbits were so plentiful in Ireland as to be a costly nuisance for farmers, so they had no objection to people coming on to their land to catch them. One of the more successful ways of doing so was by a method known locally as "rabbit-lamping". It was hard work, but by 1950, my brother Vincent and I had brought this method to a fine art. It involved going out on dark nights and shining a bright light into fields to dazzle grazing rabbits, making it easy for a dog to catch them.

The equipment needed was a headlamp from an old motorcar, and a well-charged car battery, which you carried on your back. Also needed was a good dog to catch and retrieve the rabbits without damaging them. Such a dog was hard to get. My dog, called 'Fly', was a half-greyhound, got as a pup from a traveller by the name of Moorehouse, in a swap for a ferret. I have still to do a better deal. All this hunting was done in the winter, so, to protect us from the weather, we each had a second-hand German army coat, also supplied by Mr. Moorehouse. These coats were designed for wear on the Eastern Front and did their job well, except that after a night's rain they weighed a ton.

The starting time for our rabbit-lamping varied; we worked according to the cycle of the moon. If the moon didn't rise until twelve or one o'clock, we set out about seven and hunted until it got bright. When the moon was in the sky early in the night, we went to bed and got up as soon as it disappeared, this could be three or four o'clock in the morning. We often hunted for six or seven hours a night, climbing over ditches and slogging over ploughed ground, with four stone on our backs.

There was no hunting while the moon was full, so, once a month we had a week's rest. During this week we would try to make up for lost time, pulling beet and snagging turnips, and all the other backbreaking chores around a farm. We could earn at least three times the average wage while the rabbit season lasted. In addition to the money, for me it was toughening, comparable to the gym work players do today. But it wasn't the best training for hurling, as I was to learn later.

Wexford's first game in 1951 was against Laois in the League, played in Portlaoise. Tom Dixon made his debut in this game. Wexford won, 7-02 to 4-02. Looking back on it now, it seems a strange score. Nickey Rackard had settled very well into the full forward position and was terrifying defenders; so much so that they would drag him down, and he would blast the resulting free to the net. But Artie Foley was not playing well in goal, the full back line was unsteady and, although we were scoring lots of goals, we were giving away soft goals and not scoring enough points. There were still other weaknesses, such as some players not being played in their best positions.

On 1 April 1951, we played the last game in our group of the 1950-51 National League. It was against Waterford and was played in Wexford Park. Waterford were leading by six points at half time, blurring the Statue of Liberty somewhat; but by full time she came into focus again, as we won by 3-06 to 2-06. An indication that our team-building was making progress was the fact that twelve of the team who played against Waterford that day played in and won All-Irelands four and five years later. It took all that time for us to get our act together, so, when people say the team should have won more in the interval, I would have to agree.

Only Meath now stood between us and a place in the League final so we were beginning to think winning the trip to New York was a possibility. We duly disposed of Meath and were into the final against Galway, who had come through a strong division which included Cork, Clare, Limerick and Kilkenny. They had also beaten us in the Oireachtas final, so, in a meeting with them we would be up against it.

For the first time, we went into serious training. Between the chance of a trip to America and this new type of training, the team began to feel under pressure. We did some gym work in Clonroche hall, and some hurling on a very poor field nearby. For the first time we had a masseur and a weighing scales. Big Bill Esmonde was the masseur, and the first time I got up on the bench, he said, "For God's sake, Martin, there's nothing to rub here only bones; get down and weigh yourself". I scarcely made twelve stone. "You should be at least thirteen stone", he said, and told me to drink plenty of milk and raw eggs.

Big Bill Esmonde (left) with Billy Rackard.

The problem was that I had spent four months of the winter doing ten or twelve miles every night hunting rabbits over rough country, and, to do a bit extra, every morning I had run the three miles from Rathnure, where Kitty and myself were living, down home to work the farm, and back again at night. For one who was doing manual work, I now know that was overdoing it.

The National League final of 1950-51 was played against Galway on 22 April 1951, in Croke Park. Close to thirty thousand people turned up for the game, of those, I'd say, twenty thousand were shouting for us. We started quite well: after getting an early point, Paddy Kehoe hit a line ball from forty yards out and it went all the way to the net. Padge Kehoe then sent over a point. We were now five points up and I, for one, thought to myself, this is going to be easy. I could see the Statue of Liberty in the distance, but everything changed in a matter of minutes. Between then and half time Galway scored five goals and two points. We scored a couple more points, but at the break it was Galway 5-02, Wexford 1-04. Everything that went near our goal had gone in.

After the break Artie Foley was replaced in the goal by Pat Shannon. We tried to rally, but the damage had been done and we could not get our game going. Galway out-scored us again, by 1-05 to 2-00, leaving the final score 6-07 to 3-04.

All through life, whether as a player or a spectator, I could get over a defeat very quickly if the team had played well, but the memory of this game still hurts after more than fifty years. Not one of the Wexford team could be proud of his performance that day. To say we were disappointed would be an understatement. We were shocked and ashamed; we had let our supporters down, and left a doubt in our own minds about the future.

Both the national and the local press went to town on us after this game. It was our first taste of negative press, and we were like children being scolded for the first time. Up until now it was all praise, even when we were beaten. The commentators on this occasion hinted that we hadn't tried hard enough. It was like being blamed for something we didn't do, whatever else this bunch of players did, we never threw in the towel.

I can only speak for myself and say what went wrong with my own game. I was playing on Joe Salmon, one of the best centre field men of all time, and, if I wanted to hit the big time, he was the kind of player I had to be able to handle. The puck-outs from our goal were landing short, leaving Jim Morrissey and myself at a disadvantage, unable to use our skill at overhead striking. I was stuck to the ground; I had no energy and was always that yard behind in running. Eventually, I was moved to centre forward, but the harder I tried, the worse I got - I can't remember striking one good ball. The only excuse I can make is that I had been doing too much physical training; I was two stone lighter than five years later, when I played my best hurling.

When the disappointment of the Galway game was over, it was obvious there was a lot of work to be done. The selectors did not have the necessary experience to be able to manage a team properly; and, in any case, they hadn't yet got the necessary panel of players. Artie Foley was not happy in goal. The fullback line was shaky. Billy Rackard was never right at corner back. Martin Byrne was coming to the end of a great career and was slowing down. Mick Hanlon, too, was gone thirty years of age; he could still look after his own patch, but that was all. Ned Wheeler was just out of minor grade, so he had a lot to learn. Bobby Rackard at twenty-four was reaching his peak, but needed more assistance from those around him if the team was to progress. Although there were a lot of miles on his clock, "Wilkie Thorpe" still had quite a bit to offer. Jim Morrissey and I had a disastrous game against Galway, but I think we learned from it. Paddy Kehoe was still hurling well, but his level of fitness was open to question. Tim Russell was slowing up and needed someone to win the ball for him. Dom Hearn was being played out of position, something he had to cope with during his whole inter-county career. Padge Kehoe, Tim Flood and Nickey Rackard were scoring machines; all they needed to win a game was someone to get the ball up to them. If they had a fault in the early years, it was that they each tried to do it all individually.

We had only two weeks to lick our wounds before the first round of the 1951 championship, against Meath. The game was fixed for Trim, Meath's home ground, and I remember it well - for all the wrong reasons. At first no one was too worried: Meath looked a soft thing and we could get to winning ways again. To this day I don't know whether the selectors were resting players or looking for replacements, or both, but for this game they made seven changes on the team: gone to the subs bench were "Wilkie" Thorpe, Martin Codd, Martin Byrne, Tim Russell, Paddy Kehoe, Dominic Hearn and - wait for it - one Nickey Rackard. Artie Foley was left at home! Now the papers and supporters really had something to talk about; it also made the team somewhat nervous and created a lot of tension between the mentors and some of the players.

The team to face Meath was:

	Pat Shannon	
Mick O'Hanlon	Billy Rackard	Seamus Hearne
Ted Morrissey	Bobby Rackard	Ned Wheeler
Jim Morrissey	John Cummins	
Tom Dixon	Padge Kehoe	Bob Slater
Tim Flood	Jim Quinn	Bobby Donovan

This game was the first of a few crossroads the team came to in the next two or three years. If we had been beaten, I hate to think what might have happened. As it turned out, we were lucky to play a draw in a game which might not have been finished were it not for the cool heads of two of the Meath players. Mick O'Brien and Brian Smith were experienced and respected members of the Meath football team who had won the All-Ireland in 1949, and they pleaded with their supporters to keep off the pitch in the excitement of the last few minutes.

Shortly after half time, with Meath in the lead and Wexford under pressure, Nickey Rackard began to tog off on the sideline; the Meath supporters didn't seem to like it and became a bit abusive. With tension running high, Nickey, Dominic Hearn and myself were sent on. We may not have set the game alight, but Nickey scored a goal and we got a draw out of it. The mentors may have made a bit of a mess on the occasion, but, at least, they brought three players onto the panel who later became superstars: Seamus Hearne played at centre back, where he was a disaster on the day; John Cummins was at centre field and looked promising; Nick O'Donnell was among the subs.

Apart from the two footballers, the only other Meath player I can remember from that day was their goalkeeper, a man by the name of Dick Grogan, who stood six feet five inches tall and looked very athletic. He stopped every ball that came near him, and his clearances and puck-outs were massive. We played against him again on a few occasions and he was one of the best goalkeepers I have ever seen. On our way home from Trim after the game, someone said he was a Garda, prompting the thought, if only we could get him transferred to Wexford!

The replay took place in Enniscorthy two weeks later and Wexford won more or less as we pleased, Again, Dick Grogan gave an exhibition of goalkeeping. The final score was 3-10 to 0-02, with Meath getting no score in the second half. Although we advanced to the next round of the championship, a certain feeling of doubt had entered the minds of the followers. The team wasn't consistent.

Dublin were the opposition in the Leinster semi-final and the match was played in Kilkenny. The team chosen for the occasion looked strong; still, there was a fear there that the goalkeeper and fullback line were vulnerable. Nick O'Donnell was the new fullback. This surprised the Wexford attendance because they knew very little about him. He had recently come to live in Enniscorthy and joined the St. Aidan's club. Shortly before, I had seen him play centre back for Eire Og, Kilkenny, in a challenge match against Rathnure and I wasn't impressed. I thought he looked slow. Nicko, as he later came to be popularly referred to, was about twenty six years of age at this time and had got a few runs with Kilkenny, but was deemed surplus to requirements. It is amazing that someone in Kilkenny did not notice this man's wonderful talent.

Tony Herbert was playing on Nicko that day and found him more than he could handle. Herbert, who was one of the famous Limerick family, had thrown in his lot with Dublin, but was well past his best by now, so the experts were saying, wait until Nicko meets a nippy young forward, then we'll see what he's like. The selectors were very pleased with his display, but the goalkeeper was still a problem.

When the team to play Laois in the Leinster final was announced, there was another almighty shock - Jim Rackard, a fourth member of the famous family, was in goal. Although he was twenty-six years old and had on occasion played in the goal

Jim Rackard, left, (seen here with his brothers Bobby and Nickey).

for the Rathnure club, this would be his first time to put on a county jersey. I have often been asked why Jim never made the big time like his brothers. Unlike his brothers, he was a small man, five feet eight or nine inches tall, and ten or eleven stone weight. He was a brilliant hurler, but completely different to his brothers. He was a forward with great speed and skill, who would tackle as if his life depended on it. He worked in the family pub in Killanne and seldom did I see him practise or train in Rathnure. He was a gentle, obliging man who had a huge problem with alcohol from a young age

Another addition to the panel of players at this time was an eighteen years old featherweight by the name of Jim English. The panel now included fifteen of the players who took part in the All-Irelands of '55 and '56. Things were progressing.

There was always great harmony in the camp; we were naïve and contented with how things were going. Two years earlier, a game that involved Wexford would barely get a mention in the daily press, but now that had all changed. Top sports journalists were searching for words to describe this team, words like *magnificent, majestic, talented, sporting, honest, powerful giants, bony,* but all too often accompanied by the term, *gracious in defeat.* For too long we kept ambling along enjoying the adulation of the media and the admiration of the worshipping supporters; we had not yet developed the self-belief or the hunger necessary to succeed at top level. If there had been one person with the experience and know-how to take charge, we would have won more, and sooner. It was a difficult time for the County Board officials; cash was scarce and facilities poor, but they were doing their best.

John Randall of Killurin was the official hurley maker for the team. John would give individual attention to each player's needs. He would study his style and make his hurl accordingly. Since there was no uniformity in the style of hurling played by members of this team, John believed each hurl should be different. He spent hours making a hurl for me for the 1956 final. I played the one game with it, and it is

still one of my most
treasured possessions.
I am firmly convinced
John Randall knew
what he was talking
about when it came to
making special hurls
for individual players,
and I don't think he
received enough credit
for his work.

**John Randall at work. He knew
what he was talking about when
it came to making hurls.**

A group of people who were very much part of the
travelling circus - and that is what it was - which
accompanied the team to the various venues, were the
hackney-car drivers. There was no team bus, so the County
Board hired four or five car owners to transport the team.
Most of these men were fanatical hurling men, and were
happy to carry the bags, and run with the spare hurls and
bottles of water during a match. I remember one occasion
when one of them had to go in goal for a charity match.
Another man who joined the crew about this time, too, was
Dr. Paddy Daly. A Galway man living in Killanne, he was a
friend of the Rackard family and a great GAA man. A no-
nonsense GP, players did not feign injury while Dr. Daly was
in charge.

The Leinster final of '51 was played in Croke Park on 15
July and, as usual, the Wexford supporters were present in
their thousands. This time they would not be disappointed.
The only let-down was when the team emerged from the
dressing room wearing a new set of jerseys with light blue
and yellow horizontal bands, and socks to match Gone were
the old familiar purple and gold. But the players were glad to
get the new set. The old ones were a scourge to wear because
they were made of something that felt like hair. They had no

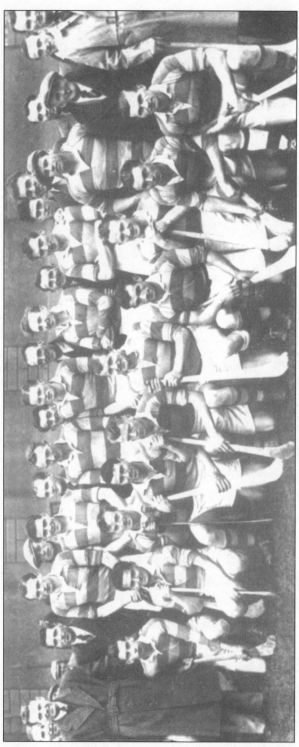

Wexford 1951 Team

Players, subs, selectors and backroom team - back row from left: Eamonn Cullen (selector), Billy Kielthy (selector), Doctor P.J. Daly (in background), Joe Bailey (selector), Bobby Rackard, Mickie Redmond (selector), Padge Kehoe, Tom Kehoe (County Secretary), Mick O'Hanlon, Martin Flood, Billy Rackard, Jim Walshe (selector), Tim Russell, unnamed supporter, Nick O'Donnell, Martin Codd, Bill Esmond (trainer), "Wilkie" Thorpe, Sean Browne (county chairman), Jimmy Leary (masseur), Des O'Neill, John Canavan (selector), front row: Paddy Kelly, Tim Flood, John Cummins, Jim Morrissey, Ned Wheeler, Nickey Rackard, Art Foley, Martin Byrne, Seamus Hearne, Dom Hearn.

collar, just a light band around the neck, and you would have a rash on your back for a week after a match.

The final score in this game was, Wexford 3-12, Laois 4-03. We had won our first Leinster final in thirty-three years, but we still needed a goalkeeper. Jim Rackard had a reasonably good game, but did not look comfortable in the unfamiliar position. Most of the team played well and enjoyed the big occasion in Croke Park, which we now considered our second home ground. When it comes to the final stages of the All-Ireland championships, I think it is always an advantage for Leinster teams to have played so much at headquarters. To win the Leinster championship after such a long wait was a huge achievement, but the celebrations had to be put on hold as the All-Ireland semi-final, against Galway, was to be played just two weeks later. Still, the county was on a high, and people who had seldom seen a hurling match were becoming experts on the game.

Everyone wanted to go to Croke Park now, but transport and money were a problem. It was sad to hear hard-working people say they hadn't the money to go to these games. My father loved hurling, but was never in Croke Park. He would say someone must stay at home and mind the house, but that was not the reason. He had many comrades.

The only change the Wexford selectors made for the semi-final against Galway was, again, to bring in a new goalkeeper. Ray Brennan, from Davidstown, was the fourth man to be given the No.1 jersey. No one seemed to know anything at all about him, except that he was playing in goal for University College, Dublin. One problem which had been solved was the puck-out. Nick O'Donnell was sending balls into the half forward line and beyond. He could also pick out a team-mate who was winning the ball, and he would never strike a ball over the sideline. These may be simple things, but they all add up. Jim Morrissey was becoming an expert on the sideline cuts; he would seldom waste one by sending it wide. Like a golfer, he would drop the ball where he wanted to, usually in front of Nickey Rackard. Slowly, each player was getting to know his own strengths and weaknesses, and using this knowledge to the advantage of the team. They all had good hurling brains and seldom did stupid things. The press and the public, from the beginning, talked about the strength and sportsmanship of the players, and this was something we became very proud of.

Galway were firm favourites to win this match, and rightly so, having already beaten us in the finals of two competitions in the past year. In Wexford we saw it differently. We now knew this Galway team, Nick O'Donnell and John Cummins were major improvements to our team, and we had a new goalkeeper. I think the attitude of some of the team and supporters at the time was that they expected to win every game, and, when we were beaten, they would say, "Well, sure, we're only coming, anyway, and what's another year?" The truth was five or six of the panel were on the thirty years mark, and time was running out for them.

Having won our first Leinster title after such a long wait, the team went into this All-Ireland semi-final very relaxed, and this was a great help. We kept with Galway, score for score, and drew level with them for the first time with about ten minutes to go. Then, Galway went ahead again when Josie Gallagher sent over a point from a free. This was to be their last score. From the puck-out, Nick O'Donnell sent a long, long ball down field to where it broke to Nickey Rackard and, as so many times before and after, Nickey shook the net. Wexford were two points in front now, and, with supporters going wild for the last few minutes, had points from Padge Kehoe, Tim Flood, and one more from Nickey Rackard, to leave the final score, Wexford 3-11, Galway 2-09.

Surely now, Wexford were in the big time. What could be

greater than playing an All-Ireland final against the champions of the past two years? There would be six weeks now to train and devise a way to beat one of the best Tipperary teams ever. People were saying, all we need now is a bit of luck and we'll be champions. In reality you need fifteen exceptionally good players, then you need the luck. Although Nick O'Donnell was developing into a great full back, everyone knew we still had problems around the goal. Jim Langton, the great Kilkenny star, was invited in to help with the preparation for the game and it was greatly appreciated that he came; but no one could supply the hunger and experience that were missing.

Everyone knew we needed help, but it just was not there. The selectors were doing their best without success to find a goalkeeper. In the space of six months, they had tried seven different men in competitive games. At that time I was finding it difficult to hold a permanent place on the team, and was asked if I would consider giving the goal a try. I did consider it, but came to the conclusion that if I failed, I, too, like the others would be gone forever. In hindsight, I should have given it a go.

The result of the final was, Tipperary 7-07, Wexford 3-09. The score was proof, if proof was needed, that we still had the same old problem: we were leaking goals. Tipperary scored four goals and one point in the second half. Every time the ball came near our goal, there was silence in the Wexford crowd; and then they would go wild again when the team went on the attack. A big disappointment was that Nickey's "specials" didn't work. Three times in the second half he was hauled down, but each time his attempt at goal was saved. This was the only time I can remember that none of them succeeded. He did score two goals from play, but was disappointed to miss three of his "specials" at vital times in the game. He always said if he scored one in three, he was breaking even - the one goal equalled the three points he could otherwise have scored.

Most of the players had played brilliantly in the final, which added to their growing reputations; but we had now been beaten in three finals - the Oireachtas, the National League and the All-Ireland - in less than a year. There were still mountains to climb and valleys to cross; no one could have anticipated how difficult and frustrating it would be to make the final breakthrough and win at least one of those trophies: there must have been times when players thought to themselves, "Is it worth all this time and effort?"

However, the loss of the All-Ireland did no harm to our popularity, or to the team itself. The supporters were magnificent in their loyalty. Many of the thousands travelling to Croke Park had a blind faith in the team. There were parts of the county where the people knew very little about hurling, but they still travelled in droves, enjoying the excitement at a time when there was very little else to get excited about. Anyone who could afford it was following the team everywhere. Since we had reached the finals of three major competitions in the past year, with a few charity matches added in, it meant we and they were on the road almost every second Sunday.

Going to the various venues, we would never see a car with two or three people in it. Vehicles that should have had only five occupants would have seven adults and perhaps a couple of young lads as well. This was to be the norm for the next few years and the players appreciated it. However, as might be expected, it created problems for some inexperienced drivers.

For all these years, Martin O'Dwyer was our driver. He had a hackney car and was the owner of a garage in Ballywilliam. He was a decent and obliging man, with great patience and a good sense of humour, all of which were needed at times.

From the time Jim English joined the panel of players, when going to Dublin we went through Bagenalstown, where Jim lived, then to Carlow and up the Naas road to the city. This was the route followed by many of the supporters from the west of the county.

Being a garage owner and a mechanic meant that Martin O'Dwyer would have problems on the way with fellows whose old bangers of cars had broken down - anything on four wheels that could move, would be on the road. Knowing that Martin would be coming along with the players, they would be on the look out for him, and since some of them would be among his best customers, he could not afford to pass them by.

I remember one day, this fellow flagged us down, Martin stopped and we all got out to have a look. There were five very worried looking middle-aged men standing around the car. Three of them were brothers and were what you might call "snug" farmers. The younger brother was the driver and he said to us, "There's nothing wrong, lads, only she stopped and won't start". Martin lifted the bonnet to have a look for the problem, while the older brother went back and opened the boot. "Begob", he said, "I thought we had everything, and there she is now and she stopped". In the boot there were three spare wheels, all with bad tyres, a five-gallon drum of water, three bottles of waste oil and a long piece of rope. After a minute or two I heard Martin say, "When was the last time you put petrol in this one, Jim?" There was a moment's silence. "Oh, Christ, lads, we never thought of the petrol. What are we going to do now?" Martin went to the boot of his car and took out a bit of hosepipe and a big bottle. He siphoned a bottle of petrol from his own car and poured it into Jim's. After two or three pulls of the starter she started up and the lads packed in. "Another satisfied customer", said Dwyer, as they disappeared up the road to Dublin in a cloud of black smoke.

The Morris Minor and the Volkswagen Beetle were the popular cars of the day and quite a few were to be seen on the roads. At this time, all you had to do to get your full driver's licence was to send ten shillings to the County Hall in Wexford and you got the licence by return of post, so you can imagine what some of the drivers were like.

There was a middle-aged man from Rathnure who bought an old Ford V8, got a hackney licence and went into business. He had no interest whatsoever in hurling and had never been much farther from home than Enniscorthy, but a few of the local lads hired him to bring them to Dublin for one of the big matches.

They decided they would start at daylight to give themselves lots of time, and everything would be grand. Not one of them had been to Dublin before, so the plan was to drive well into the city and wait in the car until they spotted the crowds going to Croke Park, and they could follow them. One man was designated to guide the driver in the city, to tell him when the traffic lights were red or green, and when to go or stop. Everything was going according to plan when they came out onto a big wide street. They had plenty of time, so they pulled into one side and parked - it was now only a matter of time, they thought, until the crowds would begin to come and they would be off again.

It was a lovely sunny day and the lads were out sitting on the car and moving about admiring their strange surroundings when they heard a band in the distance. Very soon they could see a big crowd of people coming along the street, so they got back into the car, ready for take-off. A brass band passed by, followed by groups of children and nuns, and people carrying all kinds of banners and flags, but nowhere could they see a Wexford flag or a bit of purple and gold. They came to the conclusion it was better to get going again, so, when they got a bit of space, they moved off very slowly.

Soon the children moved up on both sides of the car and it got a bit tight for the driver, so he stopped again. Now, with the car on the middle of the street and people passing on both sides, a big Garda with a Cork accent shouted,

"Are ye stayin' there all day, boy, or where are ye goin'?"

"We're goin' to Croke Park", said one of the boys.

"If so, boy, ye're goin' the wrong direction".

"We don't know the way, so we thought we'd follow the crowd".

"Yerra, boy, sure, this is a Blessed Sacrament procession. I'll make a bit o' room for ye here now; pull in to one side and we'll sort this out".

After asking a few questions and getting some stupid answers, the Garda got an escort for them and put them back on the road for home. Five very tired and hungry men got home to Rathnure that night, never again to venture out on the road to Croke Park, but they got pleasure for years from telling the story.

The achievements of the Wexford hurling team in 1950 and '51 were so spectacular and unexpected that they gave its followers a lift and a kick-start from the depression they endured in life and in hurling in the 1940s. Every time we beat one of the stronger hurling counties it was an uplifting experience, but there was still no panic about winning All-Irelands.

Two weeks after our defeat in the '51 All-Ireland final, we played Cork in the semi-final of the Oireachtas competition in Wexford Park, with another new goal man. This time it was Jim McBride from the St. Martin's club who was given his chance. After a great display, and with a fine tally of points, Wexford won with a score of 3-17 to Cork's 3-03. Kilkenny beat the All-Ireland champions Tipperary in the other semi-final, to set up another confrontation between themselves and Wexford in Croke Park.

At this point the sports journalists in Dublin were getting confused in their assessment of the Wexford team. They hadn't yet got the confidence or the courage to come out and say we were capable of beating any of the big boys. They had already forecast a Cork versus Tipperary contest for this final, and said a repeat of the Munster final would be a big money spinner for the Oireachtas people. But now, with an all Leinster final, they could only suggest that, as Kilkenny had had a quiet year, they would be fresh and eager for the game, while Wexford, who'd had a hard and frustrating season, might be tired. In choosing their team, the Wexford selectors completed the circle by putting Artie Foley back in the goal for what turned out to be a really good game of hurling.

As usual the sight of the Kilkenny black-and-amber jerseys brought the best out of Wexford, and we scored three goals and two points before Kilkenny got their first score. Slowly but surely, the Cats got back into the game and were only one point behind at half time. Shortly after the restart, Nickey scored one of his 21 yards "specials", which was to be the difference at the end: Wexford 4-07, Kilkenny 3-07. This was our first win in an Oireachtas final, a competition which had served us well over the years; it guaranteed us games against the top teams in the country, from which we gained useful experience.

The team which won the Oireachtas Cup was:

Art Foley

| Martin Byrne | Nick O'Donnell | Mick O'Hanlon |
| Sam Thorpe | Bobby Rackard | Billy Rackard |

Jim Morrissey   Ned Wheeler

| Padge Kehoe | John Cummins | Tim Russell |
| Tim Flood | Nickey Rackard | Paddy Kehoe |

Others in contention for places at this time were: Dom Hearn, Martin Flood, Seamus Hearne, Martin Codd, Ted

Morrissey, Jim English, Bobby Donovan and Ted Bolger. Of these, Jim English had not been tried.

It was now 19 October, and we still had to play four games in the 1951-52 National League before the winter break. We played Waterford in New Ross and I remember it well because the County Board had got a few pounds somewhere and purchased a lovely new set of jerseys. They were nice and soft, had a white collar with two buttons at the front, and they returned to the original purple and gold county colours. The supporters noticed the new jerseys immediately and gave the team a standing ovation. Seamus Hearne appeared again on the team. this time at wing back, not his best position. Eight and a half thousand spectators saw Wexford win by 2-09 to 1-04. Late in November we played Kilkenny in Kilkenny, and again the press men had to search for words to describe the fine hurling in a match that finished in a draw. Somewhere along the way, we beat Laois and Antrim and ended the year in a strong position.

For two months now, there would be no matches or training. This gave me time to think and meditate on what had happened to me and all the other lads in the past two years. It was the first thing on my mind in the morning and the last thing before I went to sleep. When all the players were available, I wasn't able to hold my place on the team, but, there being a few others in the same position, I wasn't too worried. Some day everything would come right and we would win an All-Ireland. Often at night, for want of something better to do, I would write down the names of the full panel of players and start picking the team myself.

One day a cattle dealer from New Ross called to our house to buy a few heifers, and he was brought in for a cup of tea. I knew this man for a few years and always considered him an expert on hurling. He was a half Kilkenny man, and you would never know whether he was with you or against you.

The conversation turned to hurling. I produced the piece of paper I had the team and subs written on, and asked, "What do you think of that team to win an All-Ireland?"

He looked at the paper for a minute and said, "You'll never win an All-Ireland with those backs."

"How do you make that out?" I asked.

"Only O'Donnell and Bobby Rackard are good enough, the others are too old and slow", he said. "Bring Bobby back on the corner and look for two good fast wing backs. The centre field is good, but Paddy Kehoe is out of place in the corner, and Tim Russell is past it." Then he said, "The subs are all centre field men".

I was disappointed with his assessment, but I couldn't argue with him as five of the subs did play in the middle of the field for their clubs. When he was gone, I wrote down what he had said on the back of the piece of paper with my team on it, and put it in the box with some other bits and pieces I was collecting. Years later, I found this piece of paper and thought to myself, how right he was.

Many of the older generation still believe the team which emerged in the early 1950s should have been more successful in winning titles. The reality is that, of the team which played in those first years, five were gone past their best and five looked promising but had still to prove they had what it takes, which left five who could hold their own in any company. Bobby Rackard, Jim Morrissey, Tim Flood, Padge Kehoe and Nickey Rackard formed the backbone on which such a team would be built. Having spent his career up to this at centre field or centre forward, Nickey had now moved with great success to full forward, where he was terrifying defences with his amazing scoring power. Some new recruits were needed, and, in time they came - from strange places in a couple of instances.

Experience was in short supply in both the team and

management. There were no team managers back then; this meant that the five individuals who picked the team also made the changes in personnel or in player positions during a game. With a limited number of senior clubs in the county, it was difficult to find men with enough experience to do the job required - it was like starting to climb Mount Everest without a Sherpa, or a guide. After many great victories and even more cruel disappointments, it was to be five years before we won our first All-Ireland. Yet, most of the people who started the journey were still there in some form or another: two of the players from 1950 became selectors and one became treasurer of the County Board.

There were times when completing the journey seemed almost impossible, but no one ever said, "We'll turn back". Each year we would meet and beat some of the best teams in the country, but we couldn't win either the National League or the All-Ireland. One of the things which kept the team going was the wonderful support of the Wexford people, but in the long term, I believe, were it not for the persistence and leadership of Nickey Rackard, this Wexford team would have failed. Building a team is like putting a jigsaw together. The difference is that with the jigsaw you start with all the pieces and you have a picture on the lid of the box of how the puzzle appears with all the pieces in place; whereas, with a hurling team you don't have all the pieces to begin with and, although you may have a dream team in your head, it won't become a reality until you find the missing pieces. In Wexford it took years to find all the pieces but, once assembled, the finished product was so unlike anything ever seen in the county before that it could only be considered a masterpiece.

1952

The Railway Cup competition was of huge interest in GAA circles in the 1950s. It was a competition played between teams from the four provinces made up of those players considered to be the best in the province, regardless of their county. It was, therefore, a great honour to be chosen to play for your province. The semi-finals were played about the first of March, and the finals on St. Patrick's Day in Croke Park.

Bobby Rackard was a regular on the Leinster hurling team and liked to do some hurling in February. As soon as we got a fine Sunday, he would say to me after Mass, come up to the hurling field in the afternoon and we'll puck a ball around for an hour or so. We'd never do any sprinting or running, just hit the ball from one to the other. We would arrange to go into New Ross for a massage. A man by the name of Kehoe who, I think, was an ex-army man, would give us a full body massage with olive oil - he had great belief in olive oil and would use nothing else. We thought it great to loosen up the muscles and get us going again after the winter break. Perhaps it was all in the head, but we had faith in what we were doing, and it worked for us.

We may not have had the hamstring problems so prevalent nowadays, but we had ailments you would never hear of now. Chilblains! Chilblains were something I used to get in the winter from working out in the cold and frost. Fingers and toes would become swollen and itchy, and sometimes the skin would crack and become sore. There were times in February and March when I would have bandages on my hands, and bits cut out of my boots to ease the pain in my toes. I often lost half a night's sleep with chilblains, but they would disappear when the weather got a bit warm.

When the selectors sat down to pick the team to face Cork in our first match of the National League in 1952, they, once

again, had to find a goalkeeper. Artie Foley was injured, so
they brought in a complete newcomer, Paddy Kelly from the
St. Fintan's Club. Seamus Hearne was retained at wing back
in place of Sam Thorpe, who was also out through injury. The
Wexford followers were still suffering from an inferiority
complex and were very worried because the press were
saying that Cork were travelling at full strength, which
meant Christy Ring would play. The last time we had played
Cork was in the Oireachtas semi-final the previous October;
Wexford had won then by fourteen points, but, according to
the experts, this time it would be different. It was a very
important contest for Wexford as a win would almost
certainly put us into the League final.

February 10, 1952, was a bitterly cold day, but the park in
New Ross was packed to capacity. It was hard to know exactly
how many people were at the game because, as well as the
people who had paid to get in, a fair few dodgers would have
come through the hedges, making the crowd close to ten
thousand. Seating in the park was almost nil, so you had the
situation where almost all the attendance were standing on
banks surrounding the pitch. Because the spectators were
uncomfortable in those circumstances, you got the feeling
they could spill onto the pitch when the excitement built up.
Broadcast commentators often remark that teams haven't
settled, but this day the teams were settled all right, it was
the spectators who hadn't settled.

As there was no television at the time, few Wexford people
would have seen Christy Ring play at centre forward for
Cork. Immediately the ball was thrown in, he moved in on
Bobby Rackard. Although the ordinary Wexford follower was
only beginning to understand the game, he knew he was
going to see something very special here. Bobby was fast
becoming the idol of the Wexford hurling world, and this was
going to be the ultimate test for him. If he could master Ring,

he could master the best, because Ring was the best.

The exchanges in the first few minutes were scary; the challenges were fair, but certainly not friendly. It seemed as if Cork were there to intimidate and put these Wexford fellows in their place once and for all. It was the wrong tactic, as, up the centre, this Wexford team was awesome: there were Nick O'Donnell, Bobby Rackard, Ned Wheeler and Jim Morrissey, John Cummins and Nickey Rackard. The average weight of those fellows was fourteen stone, and they never tried to go round anyone.

Bobby hurled with "controlled aggression", and Ring got no score. He moved off Bobby in the last quarter, and he never again looked comfortable when playing on him. Bobby always said there was no easy way to stop Ring, you could only limit him. They were two very different men, and their style of hurling was also different. They had some hard battles, but became good friends. I doubt we'll ever see their likes again.

The final score told its own story: Wexford 5-11, Cork 4-06. The result showed that this Wexford team was here to stay.

Most of the team were also pretty good footballers, with at least twelve of us having played for the county at one time or another. Paddy Kehoe, Nickey Rackard and "Wilkie" Thorpe all played for Leinster. Mick O'Hanlon and Padge Kehoe were also good and played a number of years for the county. The rest of us were late starters, which left us with one bad foot (and in some cases two!). I never met a man who could catch the ball above me, but when I came down with it, I had a fierce problem - I couldn't kick it. Bobby Rackard was twice persuaded to give the football a try, at centre back in League games, but he said you would need to be able to do more than catch the so-and-so thing.

Cross country running was another sport a few of us tried in the winter months, but only for fun. One individual took up boxing during the off season and, when asked how he got on, he said it was bad for the eyesight, that it was a sport you would need to be good at to enjoy it, and that he would stick with the hurling in future.

With Cork beaten, only Dublin stood between us and the National League final. Dublin in Croke Park were never easy, and this day it took a mighty effort to beat them. They had good players from other hurling counties, most of them very experienced men. Only a goal from a free by Padge Kehoe saved Wexford in the last few minutes.

So it was Tipperary and Wexford for the final, just as it had been in the previous year's All-Ireland final. Wexford believed they had a stronger team now, and headed for Croke Park quietly confident. The backs looked better, with Artie Foley in goal and Nick O'Donnell at full back, Wilkie Thorpe in the right corner and Paddy Kehoe a wing back.

The team was:

Art Foley

| Sam Thorpe | Nick O'Donnell | Mick O'Hanlon |
| Paddy Kehoe | Bobby Rackard | Billy Rackard |

Ned Wheeler   Jim Morrissey

| Padge Kehoe | John Cummins | Martin Flood |
| Dom Hearn | Nickey Rackard | Tim Flood. |

As always, the selectors were doing what they thought was best, but they were just changing players about, trying them in positions where they would never fit. Paddy Kehoe and Billy Rackard were great players, but were never at their best as wing backs. Martin Flood's style would never suit forward play, and Dom Hearn's speed and work rate were cramped when he was played on the corner.

The quality of every game Wexford played in now was guaranteed, and fanatical admirers were appearing from all over the country. These new-found supporters swelled attendances to record heights and we were becoming the glamour team of the '50s.

On 20 April 1952, Wexford's faithful followers again made the trip to Croke Park, only to return without a trophy. Tipperary were the All-Ireland champions for the past three years, so it was no great shame to be beaten by such an outstanding team, but the nature of the defeat was hard to take. I don't think I ever came home from a match more disappointed and worried; not that we had been beaten, but that Nickey Rackard was badly injured and it looked like the end of the road for our idol and leader.

Again it had been a tremendous game of hurling, with very little between the sides at any time. The Tipperary backs couldn't stop Nickey by fair tactics; so, three times they hauled him down. Three times, Nickey took his 21 yards "specials", and three times the ball was picked from the back of the Tipperary net. His third goal had levelled the score, but at a terrible price. As he struck the ball, his knee collapsed under him and he went down in a heap. It was obvious right away that he was in great pain as he was carried to the sideline. Never have I seen an injured player receive such an ovation on leaving the field. As the enormity of Nickey's loss and the extent of his injury were realised, the Wexford supporters became almost silent, and Croke park was like a mortuary.

The Wexford mentors changed players around and tried to regroup, but without success. Pat Stakelum sent over a point from a free, and Tipp were the winners by that single score.

Once more the press described Wexford as the gallant losers, but the big worry now was Nickey Rackard's knee. For years he had had a troublesome knee and sometimes wore a heavy bandage on it. It was not unusual for him to pull up abruptly in a match and, after some delicate manoeuvres and one heavy jolt to the knee, he would carry on as if nothing had happened. It seemed something dislocated in the knee and he could put it back in place himself. For weeks after the

League final everyone in the county was talking about Nickey's knee - would he ever play again? Or was he going to be a cripple for life?

There was no team from Ulster entered in the 1952 championship, so the winners of Leinster got a bye to the All-Ireland final, which meant if Wexford could win two games, we would go straight into the final. People were saving their money in expectation of having a very exciting summer. Anyone who could get a few pounds together bought a car, hoping they would need it for the matches. People with some driving experience got a free lift to Dublin as many of the new car owners would not chance driving that journey. The elderly parish priest or a wealthy old farmer were usually a good touch for such a lift; although I knew one such parish priest who set off to a match on his own, and when asked the following day how he had got on with the traffic lights in Dublin, he said, "What lights?"

Wexford was drawn to play Kilkenny in the Leinster semi-final, on Sunday 8th June, and without Nickey, our chances looked slim. Still we had made good progress in the past year and had played some great hurling, so we should be able to absorb the loss of one man. The team had two months to prepare for the game, but the foremost question was, with Nickey missing, who would do the extra scoring. There was great speculation as to how the team would be placed, and who would play full forward.

When the team was announced, there was just one change of personnel; Tim Russell came in at wing forward. Martin Flood was moved to centre forward, and John Cummins went to full forward in Nickey's place. Billy Rackard was in the full back line, and "Wilkie" Thorpe at right wing back

Kilkenny had not won the All-Ireland since 1947, and were under pressure to get back to where they always believe they belong - at the top. Wexford's supporters were blind to reality, they thought it was just a matter of time before we won the big one. They had seen their team beaten in the All-Ireland final and two National League finals in the past twelve months, but it had no effect on them at all - they were on a roll and nothing was going to stop them. Luckily, the team did not share their foolishness, especially against Kilkenny, who were always well prepared for the important game.

The fact that Wexford did not have much success in their search for a goalkeeper in the past year had not gone unnoticed in Kilkenny. From the first sound of the referee's whistle, they bombarded the Wexford goal. They neglected to take their points, to such an extent that they scored only one, and that from a free. Even though Kilkenny scored five goals, Art Foley had a fine game and saved a rasper in the final minute to leave Wexford in

John Cummins, a great loss when he emigrated in 1953.

front at the end, 4-07 to 5-01. We were into another Leinster final after a fast and furious match in which every Wexford man played his part, none more so than John Cummins at full forward, who won the "Sports Star of the Week" award in the *Irish Independent*.

Meanwhile Nickey Rackard had got a repair job done on his knee and was on his way back to full fitness, so we were going to have a surplus of good forwards. Dublin had beaten Meath by nineteen points and Laois by ten points to reach the Leinster final, which, for the first time, we were firm favourites to win. Everyone in the county was talking about hurling now, and, as the saying goes, most of them were talking through their hats. Even fellows who should have known better were so sure we would beat Dublin that their only concern was who would come out of Munster to meet Wexford in the All-Ireland. And they were wondering if the long lay-off after the Leinster final, while waiting for the All-Ireland, would be to Wexford's disadvantage.

Over thirty-eight thousand people arrived in Kilkenny for the game, the vast majority, as usual, from Wexford. It was a warm sunny day and there was a carnival atmosphere about the place; even the dressing room was relaxed and noisy. Two years earlier, in the same dressing room, we were very nervous and almost frightened before we went out to play Kilkenny in the Leinster final. What a difference a couple of years had made! To add to Wexford's confidence, it was announced just before the start that Dublin would be without three of their best players. Norman Allen, Mick Hassett and Des Dillon were missing, and surely now, Dublin had no chance - or so it was thought.

With the passing of time, I have forgotten most games in which we were beaten, and great games we have won have become greater, but this day will stick in my memory for ever, and for all the wrong reasons. The play started quiet enough, but Dublin scored a quick goal which should have shocked Wexford into action. It could have been the heat, but the first half never seemed to get going. It was stop - start, with Wexford doing just enough to lead at halftime by 2-05 to 2-01. No one was too worried, thinking the second half would be different. Sure enough, it was different, but not in the way we expected. Just as Kilkenny had done in the semi-final, Dublin were concentrating on the goalkeeper and were playing some rough stuff in around the goal. Artie Foley was injured and had to retire. He was replaced by Paddy Kelly. It was not all Paddy's fault, but Dublin scored five goals and one point in the second half, while Wexford scored only one goal and one point.

It only needed a look at the final score, 7-02 to 3-06, to realise we still had trouble in the backs. The forwards got plenty of the ball, but their shooting was way off target. After a game like this, to say a team had been over-confident, I think, is wrong, "careless" is a more appropriate word, and every Wexford person who came to Kilkenny that day was careless and paid the price. If this team and its officials had not been such a united and dedicated collection of individuals, I think this would have been the end of the dream. Instead of viewing it as the disaster it was, we treated it as another lesson learnt, and a very important one, too. Never again were we beaten by an inferior team.

It was certainly the blackest day in the history of this Wexford team. The events of that day still hurt and haunt those who were present to witness them. Still there is one small incident that I remember from that occasion which will always bring a smile to my face. All the new car-owners and drivers who had come to Kilkenny that day from Wexford drove their cars as far as possible into the city and parked them, bumper to bumper, on both sides of the road. No one thought of turning the car to face for home before parking it. This resulted in confusion after the game, when some of these inexperienced drivers attempted to turn the car to go home. Many of them got into a position where they could neither go forward nor back, with the result the road was blocked.

A group of us from Rathnure were standing on the pavement, all looking very sorrowful, when an elderly lady who was sitting in her car asked, "Has there been an accident?" No one made any move to answer her, so she shouted a bit louder, "Has there been an accident?" There was a man with us by the name of Nickie Blackburn and he moved slowly across the street to where the woman was. Nickie was a man getting on in years, but very witty and he could always see the brighter side of things. Answering the lady's question he said, "I don't know if it was an accident or not Ma'am, but a lot of people are very hurt, and what should have been a very enjoyable day has turned into a funeral". "Oh, my God!" the lady said, "Will the cortege be passing this way?" "Oh no, ma'am", Nickie said, "there's no cortege, no hearse, the corpse is Wexford hurling - just a sad, sad funeral back to Wexford", and with that, he turned and left the lady more confused than ever.

A month later, in their build-up to the All-Ireland final, Dublin came to Enniscorthy to play Wexford in a practice match, and, even with their full squad of players, each competing for a place on the team for the All-Ireland, they went home beaten, 5-08 to 2-02, a fifteen point drubbing. In the All-Ireland, Cork beat Dublin by thirteen points, and Wexford's faithful followers were left lamenting what might have been.

Just one week after the debacle against Dublin, the team came together in Wexford Park to play Kilkenny for a set of gold medals. The game was to celebrate 50 years of Feis Carman (Wexford Feis). As the organisers presumed we would be Leinster champions by now, the game got a lot of publicity. Kilkenny had promised to send their full team, and they kept their promise. The medals were very valuable. I don't know if Kilkenny knew this, but we did and we were determined to win them. Several thousand people paid to see the contest, and it was a comfort to the team to know our fans had not forsaken us. Encouraged by this, every one of the team played well, and won with something to spare.

Two months later, we played against Tipperary in the semi-final of the Oireachtas competition in New Ross. Every member of the squad was there again, ready for action, and, as usual, the spectators were crammed into the park; seeing the support for the home team must have been intimidating for teams coming to play Wexford in Wexford. Being a member of the team now, made you feel as if you owed the people something, and if you had any pride at all, you gave everything you were able. For those still worried about Nickey's knee, this game put their minds at ease. He was back at his brilliant best, and scored four goals and two points. Artie Foley had a good game in goal and proved he was an outstanding goalkeeper if he was in the right frame of mind. Wexford won, 4-06 to 3-03.

The Oireachtas final of 1951-52, against Galway, was played in Croke Park on 19 October '52, before an attendance of over thirty thousand vocal fans, who were entertained by a great game. Again, the sports journalists were searching for words to describe a match which was played at a furious pace. Mitchel Cogley, a very respected sports journalist, wrote: *If you took the highlights of all the games you ever saw and put them together, it would give you some idea of the quality of this game.* Galway were a great team and they won by three points.

It was becoming evident at this time that there was something missing in the whole Wexford set-up. We now had in the team at least ten players who were as good as any who ever played in Croke Park, but we were still content just to be pleasing the crowd. Being beaten by two or three points didn't seem to affect us at all. Pressure and hunger were still a long way off, and, not only the players, but the followers, too, were enjoying the admiration and praise. It was going to take more than fifteen good hurlers to win championships, but few in Wexford realised this at the time.

We played Laois in Gorey in the first game of the new League and won easily. In mid-November, we went to Dungarvan to play Waterford in what was always a difficult fixture. As well as being a dark and overcast afternoon, I think the game started a bit late and, by the time it was over, it was almost dark. The park in Dungarvan at that time was known as Fraher's Field, and there were some very high trees at the back of one of the goals. When the ball went in around this goal in the last few minutes, it was hard to know what exactly was going on in there. Some lads were pulling in good time, others pulling a bit late, and half the time the referee couldn't see the ball, so I think he was going on sound. One of our corner backs was asked on the way home, what was going on in there in the end, and he said, "Well, half the time we couldn't see the ball, and, although it might be gone wide, we'd hurl away for a minute or two, just to make sure". Anyway, we were beaten 3-08 to 3-06.

Our last game in 1952 was in Belfast, against Antrim. We travelled up on Saturday and came home on Monday. I remember this trip for some very different reasons.

It was the end of November and very cold, with some snow on the pitch. The match was played in the old Corrigan Park and there were shallow ridges, about six feet wide, across the pitch. Now, the snow on the top of these ridges had melted and had collected as slush three inches deep in the hollows. The dressing room was like a fridge, so, as it was not a day for hanging around, we togged off and got out on the pitch as quickly as possible. It was a few minutes later before the Antrim team and the referee arrived. Meanwhile, we were standing on top of the ridges to keep our feet dry. The coin was tossed, the backs went back to their positions, and we were ready to go when it was announced that there would be a minute's silence in memory of the great Cavan footballer, John Joe O'Reilly, who had died that week.

Then, from the loudspeaker over the dressing rooms, came that distinctive crackly hissing sound you got when you put a record on an old-time gramophone. I thought we were going to hear our national anthem, but that wasn't so - it was not permissible to play it publicly in that part of the country.

What we did hear was like thunder. It was the wonderful bass voice of the black American singer, Paul Robeson, singing the ballad, "Kevin Barry". I don't suppose many people have heard this wonderful recording, but, if you were in any way patriotic, it would make the hair stand on the back of your neck. To hear it boom out over the rooftops of Belfast was special, and we stood to attention as never before. By the time the song ended, my boots were almost stuck to the ground with frost, but I felt better, and the blood was flowing faster through my veins.

The game itself was a miserable bore, with the ball getting stuck in the slush and muck, and everyone wet and cold. We won on the score 4-08 to 2-05. During the game I was getting great shots of pain on my right side, just over my kidney, and it got worse as the game went on. We didn't have a doctor with us, but Nickey Rackard, who was a vet, had a look at me and discovered I had two broken ribs. They were the two small floating ribs, and when he pressed on them, he could feel where they were broken. I had got this injury the previous Sunday playing against Kilkenny in Arklow, where a new park was being opened. It was not very painful, except when I turned a certain way.

We had never before played in such bad conditions and were glad to get back to our hotel for a wash and a hot meal. The Antrim County Board had organised some entertainment and a céili for us on that Sunday night. There was a céili band and a singer or two, and a fine troupe of Irish dancers. These girls were all in the sixteen to eighteen age group and looked very smart in their green and yellow dancing costumes. It soon became evident, too, that they were admirers of this fine bunch of Wexford manhood. Although some of the lads could show fine footwork in Croke Park, when it came to the "Siege of Ennis" or "The Stack of Barley", their footwork left a lot to be desired. Billy Rackard and myself had learned a reel and a hornpipe while at school in Rathnure, but that was ten years ago. Still it was a help.

We could all get by with the Old Time Waltz, and things were going fine until a "Ladies Choice" for the Siege of Ennis was called. All the young girls charged across the floor to claim a dancing partner. You either got up to dance now, or you were shamed forever. To tell the truth of the lads, they all made the effort and, although it was a bit embarrassing at first, they soon got the hang of the thing and it was a great laugh.

I wasn't so lucky. My partner was a big strong girl, with a lovely good-natured smile, and she loved to dance. In no time we were going great guns and she was getting very confident. We had done two or three swings and my ribs were standing up to the pressure, but when the time came for the final swing, she flung her arm across my ribs and really went for it. This time my ribs let a crack, and I nearly went through the floor. I had to go and sit down; the sweat came out on my brow and I couldn't catch my breath.

Not knowing what had gone wrong, the poor girl came and sat down beside me. When I got my breath back, I told her I had two broken ribs and was finished dancing for the night. She was very worried. We talked for a while. She asked me about all the lads on the team, and I was surprised she knew so much about us. She was asking what age everyone was; I told her I was twenty-two and married, with two young children. She told me she had three brothers and one sister, and that she was still going to school. Then she asked me to come and meet her mother, who was working in the kitchen at the back of the stage.

There were three women in the kitchen. One of them was a nurse who told me I could develop pneumonia very quickly, or even get a punctured lung, from my broken ribs. These women said they would love to meet more of the team, so I went back to the hall to see if I could get a few of my mates, but only three would come with me. We got tea and cake, but missed our lift back to the hotel. We had played our last match for 1952, and each of us would go our own way now for two months or so. It was a cold, dry night as we walked back to our hotel. We were tired, but happy.

1953

Liam Murphy, a Cork man living in Rosslare, succeeded Tom Kehoe of Wexford town as secretary of Wexford County Board in 1953. Chosen as selectors for the senior hurling team were Tom Kehoe of New Ross, Tom Butler of Adamstown, Patsy Boggan of Piercestown St. Martins, Eamonn Cullen of Cloughbawn and Nickey Rackard of Rathnure. 1953 began on a high note but was eventually to become a year in which the team and its followers were to experience a variety of highs and lows greater and more extreme than any we had experienced so far.

Our first outing was on 1 February in New Ross. It was a League game against Kilkenny and the team selected was:

Artie Foley

Sam 'Wilkie' Thorpe   Nick O'Donnell   Mick O'Hanlon

Paddy Kehoe   Bobby Rackard   Billy Rackard

Jim Morrissey   Ned Wheeler

Padge Kehoe   John Cummins   Martin Flood

Dom Hearn   Nickey Rackard   Tim Flood.

The park in New Ross had been closed for renovations and was being reopened for this game. Formerly known as 'Barrett's Park', it was now being renamed "O'Kennedy Park", to honour the great Sean O'Kennedy, a member of the Wexford All-Ireland hurling team of 1910, and captain of the 1915-18 All-Ireland football team.

If there was any doubt in the minds of the Wexford players that their followers might be getting discouraged and tired of going to all their games, this day set our minds at ease. It was the first time I had my own car to take me to a game and I may have been late leaving home, with the result that, because of the crowd, I had to walk the last mile to the park - ten thousand fans were crammed into the field by the time I arrived. For a League match on the first day of February, this must have been a record attendance.

Artie Foley was missing on the day, so Jimmy Deegan of New Ross took his place in goal. So as not to disappoint the crowd, Wexford played as if it was an All-Ireland final and never let up from start to finish. Kilkenny may not have been up for the game to the same extent we were, but Wexford were frightening on the day and won, 7-10 to 1-02.

If there had been one man with the experience and vision to take command of the team at this time, I'm sure we would have won four All-Irelands in a row. Instead, what we were doing in every game was trying to entertain, as if that was more important than winning. All the players were honest and very sporting on the field, and this won us many friends and admirers, not alone in Wexford, but all over the country. However, after entertaining the sporting public, giving the sports journalists new material to work on, and filling the coffers of the GAA for three years, we were no nearer to winning an All-Ireland hurling championship. In hindsight, I think what we needed was a bit of professionalism, a familiar word nowadays, but unheard of in GAA circles in the '50s. Those were the days when a place on the team, whether at parish or county level, was every player's ambition, how he was treated by the officials of his club or county was secondary to that. As a team we had no complaints, we were well fed and were always collected and returned to our homes when training and on the days of games.

The first major shock we had was early in the year. Bobby Rackard had been having a problem with his nose which was affecting his breathing, so he arranged to have what was considered to be a small operation. He decided to have the procedure done after the Railway Cup final, in which he was playing on St. Patrick's Day. This would give him time to recover and be fit again for the championship. I knew he was having this operation, but put no pass on it until I went to the

April meeting of the Rathnure hurling club.

When I went into the room where the meeting was being held, there were five or six of the committee present, but the place was like a morgue. Everyone stared at me for a few seconds, and then someone said, "Did you hear about Bobby?" I said, "No. What about him?" There was one man there from Killanne, he spoke up and said, "Bobby is very sick; the whole family came home there this evening".

For the first time in my life, I went into shock as a thousand thoughts jammed my brain. As the remainder of the committee came into the room, they all had different stories. No one knew what exactly was going on, so the chairman said he would go over to Killanne and find out what the true story was.

He was back in less than half an hour, and the news was very bad. He was only allowed in as far as the front yard, where he was told how Bobby, having returned home after the operation, had developed a blood clot. He had to be kept lying motionless, and was told not to even blink an eyelid. He had collapsed completely and was being attended by two doctors. The family had all been called home, as his chances of survival were less than fifty-fifty.

Scarcely a word was spoken in the meeting room for five minutes or so as we struggled to come to terms with what we had heard. I cannot recall any occurrence in my lifetime that had shocked me more. There were about twelve men at this meeting, which was being held in a room off the bar of Conran's pub in Rathnure. When the barman came in and saw the state we were in, he went back to the bar and returned with large whiskeys for three or four of the older lads. The business of the hurling club was never mentioned again that night, but someone suggested we should say a few prayers, and at least two rosaries were recited before we left for our homes.

When I got home with the bad news, my mother, who never expressed any interest in hurling, got the rosary beads and we prayed again. I got very little sleep that night, and, as we had no telephone, I went up to Rathnure for Mass in the morning and to get the news of Bobby. Half the people of Rathnure were at Mass, and the news was a little better. Bobby had got through the night and the doctors thought he had turned a corner. A few days later, when the doctors thought it was safe to do so, he was taken back to hospital in Dublin and remained there for some weeks.

When he returned to Killanne, he was only a shadow of the man we knew as Bobby Rackard, and the story was he would never play hurling again. To make a long story short, it took more than a year before Bobby declared himself fit to play again. And it's testimony of the man's character that, four months after his return, he gave an exhibition of hurling the like of which was never seen before or since.

I am not sure that Bobby's problem was the result of an injury he received while hurling, but it made me think about my own situation. If I got a bad injury, it would leave my family in a very vulnerable position. Kitty was expecting our third child, and I had two young brothers who were still going to school. My father was seventy years old, which left me the principal breadwinner on a farm of less than a hundred acres.

I gave this a lot of thought for the next week or two, and one day, while working in the field with my father, I told him I was thinking it might be best if I gave up playing for the county team. He looked shocked and asked, "Why would you want to do that?" I said I might get hurt and not be able to work for months. "You could get hurt working here any day", he said, "and what's more, hurling is not nearly as dangerous as working with horses or catching cattle, so forget about it". He went on to tell me how privileged I was, and how proud all my relatives were of me, and that he thought it would be wrong for me to give it up now. Knowing my father as a man who never said too much, and certainly would never flatter anyone with this kind of talk, his words took me by surprise and gave me another reason to carry on playing. It's a great boost to a player to know that his family and friends and every supporter of the team are one hundred per cent behind him when he goes out on the field.

When the Wexford football team was selected to play the first round of the championship against Laois in April '53, five men from the hurling team were selected to play, and two more were subs. It is worth noting that this football team went on to contest the Leinster final that year and were beaten by Louth. It may or may not have been a harm to the hurling, but most of us involved came to the conclusion that you cannot play both games at the highest level and be successful. There was still a lingering thought in the minds of the people from the traditional football parishes that our best chance of winning an All-Ireland was in football, but, by the end of the year, the players had their minds made up that our future was in hurling, and there was no turning back.

With Bobby Rackard gone from the scene, it was accepted that the hurling selectors would have to make a few adjustments to the team for the first round of the Leinster championship, also against Laois. Well, to say there were a few surprises would be putting it mildly. It was suggested by one of the local papers that the names had been pulled from a hat. One interesting inclusion was a young lad by the name of John Mitchell from the St. Aidan's team in Enniscorthy, who was brought in at half back. [John played two or three games in '53 and then went missing until he came back and played on the team that won the All-Ireland in 1960.] The team selected played well and beat Laois by eleven points, so the critics had to stay silent.

When the team to play Kilkenny in the Leinster final was announced, all hell broke loose and the critics went to town on the selectors. The team selected was:

Art Foley

Sam Thorpe   Nick O'Donnell   Mick O'Hanlon

John Mitchell   Ned Wheeler   Billy Rackard

Jim Morrissey   Martin Codd

Tim Flood   John Cummins   Dom Hearn

Sean Flood   Nickey Rackard   Tom Dixon

On the subs bench were, Paddy Kehoe, Padge Kehoe, Seamus Hearne, Jim English and Tom Ryan.

The Kilkenny team was:

Raymie Dowling

Jim Hogan   P. 'Diamond' Hayden   Mark Marnell

Paddy Buggy   Jimmie Heffernan   Johnny McGovern

Willie Walsh   John Sutton

Sean Clohessy   Dan Kennedy   Dick Carroll

Jimmy Langton   Shem Downey   Mickey Kelly.

On paper this looked a great team, capable of winning an All-Ireland, which Kilkenny had not done since 1947. Close on forty thousand hurling fans made the trip to Croke Park, the vast majority of them optimistic Wexford supporters, but again, we were the "gallant losers", the final score being Kilkenny 1-13, Wexford 3-05. Nickey missed a 21 yard free when he failed to lift the ball, and two seventies were missed near the end. Padge Kehoe, Jim English and Tom Ryan were all brought on as subs that day. It was of little comfort to the Wexford team and our supporters to find the pressmen on the following Monday saying it was the best Leinster final in twenty years.

Cork, Kilkenny, Galway and Wexford were the teams chosen to play in the '53 Oireachtas competition. Cork, who had won the All-Ireland championship, withdrew, and Clare took their place. Wexford was fixed to play Kilkenny in

**Tom Ryan with two hurls - "a messer and a schemer", someone is
short a hurl.**

Nowlan Park on 21 September, and again, the supporters
were on the road in their thousands.

Tom Ryan had come on as a substitute in the Leinster
final, but it was in this game that he first played the full hour
at corner forward, and things were never to be the same
again around the goal. A native of Kilkenny, twenty-seven
years of age and battle-hardened, he had recently taken up
employment in Enniscorthy. He joined the St. Aidan's hurling
club, but few gave him any chance of making an impact at
inter-county level. He was big and strong, not very fast, but
dangerous in more ways than one. He was a messer and a
schemer, but there was always something intelligent in what
he was doing. He never expected or wanted to be a match-
winner, but seldom did he fail to score a goal or two.

Before Tom's arrival on the scene, Nickey Rackard, and to
a lesser extent Tim Flood, got more than their fair share of
"attention" from opposing backs. Tom soon changed all that.
He was a warrior and for him every game was a war to be
won; some wars were won by cunning and trickery, others by
all out warfare. His secret weapon was his ability to do the
unexpected. He was given the task of getting the backs'
attention away from Nickey, of acting as a decoy, and he did
this in his own inimitable way. I still remember his first move
in this Oireachtas semi-final against Kilkenny.

It was the time when the forwards lined up at centre field for the throw-in of the ball to begin the game. Tom was the first player to break from the line. Straight down the field he ran, never looking to see where the ball had gone, but looking straight at the goalkeeper. The corner back met him with a good hefty shoulder before he got to the square. Tom took no notice, just continued on his way until he got to the goal line.

He took a good look up at the crossbar, and at the net; he then walked by the goalpost and gave it a good belt with his hurl. That done, he took up a position on the corner of the square, with the corner back stuck in behind him. The ball may have been at the other end of the field, but Tom's game-plan had started. He was getting the full attention of his marker, which left Nickey Rackard with only one man to beat. The final score in the game was Wexford 3-11, Kilkenny 3-09, and Tom Ryan had scored all three Wexford goals. Some people said he was lucky on the day, that he would never get the same chances again. Others said he was a bit of an idiot and would be an embarrassment to the team; but those who mattered knew he was no fool, he just acted like one sometimes. Another cog had been fitted to the wheel, and Tom Ryan was there to stay.

Clare had beaten Galway in the other semi-final, so Wexford and Clare were to meet in a hurling match for the first time in fifty-six years. A crowd of over twenty thousand came to Croke Park on 25 October to see this extraordinary pairing do battle. Clare had won the National League six years before; therefore we knew they were going to be no pushover. There were close to twenty marching bands in the Park that day, and the sound of their music added greatly to the occasion.

The Wexford selectors were now reasonably happy with their panel of players, but they kept changing them about, as if trying to get the best blend. Against Kilkenny they had

**Jim English had a great understanding with Billy Rackard. In this
picture Billy breaks the ball down and Jim is on his way to clear.**

played Padge Kehoe at centre back in an effort to replace
Bobby Rackard. For this game they put Padge back in the
forwards and placed Billy Rackard at centre back. Jim
English, a young and physical lightweight, had come in as a
sub in the Leinster final; he was now introduced to play at
right halfback beside Billy, a position he was to hold without
a break for ten years. He had been a brilliant minor and had
been on the senior panel for two years, but wasn't given a
chance to prove his worth. It was thought that at five feet
nine inches and only ten stone weight, he was too small, but
he was a real "live-wire". He was twenty years old now and,
I'd say, at least one year of his career was lost. He and Billy
had been playing in these positions for their club, Rathnure,
and had developed a great understanding of each other's
play.

Seldom in this match did the ball pass the Wexford
halfback line, and with Tom Ryan causing confusion and
turmoil in the Clare fullback line, Wexford led by 4-08 to 1-02
at half time. One of the Clare backs had lost his cool with
Ryan and was sent off. Clare got some scores in the second
half, but Wexford won by nine points.

After this the Dublin press were again going over the top with praise for the Wexford team: one much-respected journalist even forecast that, with a bit of luck, Wexford would be All-Ireland champions in 1954. This kind of talk had a strange effect on our followers, and I think it got to the players, too. Kilkenny beat us in the first game of the National League, and Dublin came to Enniscorthy with a very strong team and gave a drubbing to a poor Wexford selection; Art Foley and a few of the regular backs were missing, with the result that Dublin scored eight goals. However, no one was too worried; we knew that the men were there now for every position, and there was more than hope that Bobby would be back for the championship. One of the positive developments from the League games was the relocation of Seamus Hearne to centrefield, where he became a different and much better player: he was never at ease in the full back line.

With the exception of Mick Morrissey, the Wexford mentors now had the panel of players who would bring the team to the next three All-Ireland finals. We were out of the '53 championship from mid-July, which gave the players and everyone involved with the team a chance to take their minds off the inter-county competitions and recharge their batteries. Two or three of the older lads decided it was time to retire, and they left the scene. However, there was plenty of action at club level. The Rathnure players were involved in three county finals that year. The '52 football final, which we won, was played in May '53, but we were beaten in both '53 county finals, hurling and football.

Even though we won nothing except the Oireachtas Cup in 1953, a number of things happened which affected the progress of the team in different ways. The most significant of these was that Nickey Rackard changed his lifestyle completely, and I'm firmly convinced that if this change had not taken place, there would have been no "glorious '50s" for

Wexford hurling, and I would not be telling this story.

From the time he went away to college in Dublin, Nickey was regarded as a heavy drinker, and many of his friends later told me they were amazed at how well he could play after a hard night's drinking. For some reason, in 1952, he decided to give up drinking completely. It may be that he came to the conclusion that he had to make one final sacrifice to achieve his sporting ambition, as he was now thirty years old and time was running out. My own belief is different.

I believe he gave up drinking because that was the dying wish of his great friend and admirer, Fr James Quigley, who was curate in Kilmyshal at the time. Fr Quigley was a serious follower of Wexford hurling, and especially of his native club, Rathnure. The story told is, when Fr James was dying of cancer, he gave Nickey his Pioneer Total Abstinence badge and asked him to give up drinking for his own sake and for the sake of Wexford hurling. Nickey wore the badge for the next five years. Fr. Quigley died at the age of fifty-two. He was born in the parish of Rathnure and was an uncle of the famous Quigley brothers who later played hurling for Wexford. Nickey and a few others of the team got married in 1953, and that, too, was a help.

Most of the team, selectors and County Board officials had now been working together for four years. They were a solid group who had come a long way and gained great experience, and were now committed to one objective, to win an All-Ireland final for themselves, their families and the people of Wexford. We had played and beaten the best teams on more than one occasion. We knew the strengths and weaknesses of every great player in the country, and Croke Park was like our home venue. We suffered one big loss at this time when John Cummins, of Horeswood, emigrated to England. He had been playing great hurling at centre forward and would be hard to replace. Two of the stalwarts from the beginning, Wilkie Thorpe and Tim Russell, decided to retire at the end of 1953. Tim became a selector for 1954, so his experience was not lost to the team.

1954

With any hope of being involved in the final stages of the National League now gone, our focus was on the championship. Because our team had got so much exposure in the national press and on radio in the past four years, there were now people in every county who were our dedicated followers. Especially in counties with no senior hurling team of their own to support, Wexford became their adopted heroes, and people from these counties were coming to our games in droves. No team had ever before stirred the popular imagination in the same way, and not just of hurling people.

Once, in the late sixties, I was visiting a friend in the midlands and he said to me, "Will you come down to the pub for an hour? There's a few lads there who would like to meet you". This pub was rural and old, and so were the people in it. There was a flagstone floor, the counter was high and painted black. The light was poor and seats were scarce, but the place was warm and homely. Eight or ten men were there, leaning on the counter with their pints.

When we entered, they all turned to say "Good night", and then continued with their chat, with one exception. This fellow kept looking at me with a quizzical smile on his face. "You're one of the Wexford hurlers", he said. I kept looking at him, but said nothing. "You're not Morrissey, or you're not Kehoe". Then he pointed his finger at me, "You're the fellow with the black curly hair and the funny name". With that, he pointed to a big framed photo hanging high on the wall. To my amazement, it was the Wexford team of '56, in all its glory.

By now, every one in the place claimed to know who I was, and, after hearing some of their comments, I asked what the attraction of that Wexford team was. Again, they talked about different players and different games, until the man behind the counter, who was old and had said very little, looked at me and, with a faraway look in his eyes, he said, "By God, I'd go to Croke Park again next Sunday if it was only to see those men march around the field, and the way they'd stand for The Soldier's Song!". He never mentioned the hurling!

The spring of 1954 was cold and wet, which left work on the farm four or five weeks behind schedule. We were still doing the tilling with horses and, as they could only work so many hours in the day, much of the crops were not sowed until May. This left me with very little time for hurling or training, but I didn't feel I was letting anyone down as there was now a surplus of centre field men, and that was the only position I felt happy in - I'd train when I could and I'd do my best if I was needed.

The news from Killanne was that Bobby was working hard on the quiet, and it was possible he would be back for the championship. If he was back to his best, what a boost it would be for the team! He was now twenty-seven years old and hadn't played a game for more than a year. To expect him to come in at top level and play well was pushing it, but those close to him never doubted his resolve.

Our first game in the 1954 championship would not take place until 6 June, in Croke Park, which allowed us plenty of time to prepare. Our opponents, Kilkenny, were firm favourites with the press to win, not alone the Leinster, but the All-Ireland title as well. Leinster had won the Railway Cup and Kilkenny had nine players on the team; Wexford had only three, so our chances looked slim enough.

Kilkenny had won their first All-Ireland in 1904 and, to celebrate the 50th anniversary, they planned to win their thirteenth this year. When they were drawn against Wexford in the Leinster semi-final, they were happy enough as Wexford had had some bad results in the League. The attitude in Wexford was, you may as well meet them first as last, the bigger they come, the harder they fall. Until now, Wexford players were content with putting on a big show and entertaining the public, but that was changing. From now on, it was going to be about winning. The hunger previously missing was there now, and each man was confident and prepared to take on his responsibility.

There was a big build-up for this clash between Wexford and Kilkenny, with the pressmen saying that the hurling power had now shifted from Munster to Leinster. This was because Leister had won the Railway Cup for the first time in thirteen years.

One of the papers read; *With nine players on the provincial team, Kilkenny should win with a bit to spare; but battling Wexford will make it a great game. Many of the Wexford team are gone past their best and may not be able for an hour of championship hurling. This may be Wexford's final kick, but what pleasure they have given to their wonderful supporters.*

These were the comments we had to read for a week before the game, but Wexford people saw things differently, especially the team and its mentors, who knew that the team was never as strong, with every man capable of holding his own in any company. Their poor performance in the League had given outsiders the wrong impression, and that was good.

The selectors for the year were Tom Butler, Nickey Rackard, Tim Russell, Nick Bowe and Patsy Boggan. Kevin Sheehan, of Enniscorthy, an army sprint champion, was trainer. The team was:

	Art Foley	
Billy Rackard	Nick O'Donnell	Mick O'Hanlon
Jim English	Bobby Rackard	Bobby Donovan
Jim Morrissey		Seamus Hearne
Padge Kehoe	Ned Wheeler	Dominic Hearne
Tom Ryan	Nickey Rackard	Tim Flood

Peter Barron of Rathnure was the new sub goalie.

This was the best team yet, and everyone was confident they would do well. Bobby Donovan was a surprise choice at wing back as he had always played in the forwards previously. Sunday, 6 June, was a miserable, wet day, which kept the crowd small, just seventeen thousand, but, as always, Wexford supporters were in the majority. The rain eased somewhat before the game began, but there was still a lot of water on the pitch.

Wexford appeared the more hungry and started off at a ferocious pace. Scores were hard to come by, but they were leading at half time. All eyes were on Bobby Rackard's every move. He looked frail and was having difficulty staying on his feet in the terrible conditions in the first half. Tom Ryan seemed happy enough as he splashed in the water in front of the goal. Nickey Rackard seeming fitter and faster than usual, roamed way out the field, taking the ageing full back, Diamond Hayden, with him. The only worry Wexford had at half-time was the scoreboard, which read 1-05 to 0-06. Kilkenny had scored only one point from play, but were still only two points behind. We need not have worried, everything changed dramatically after the break. The ground had improved a little, making it easier for the players to stay on their feet and handle the ball.

We got off to a flying start when, after just two minutes, Jim Morrissey took a sideline cut from about sixty yards out and it went all the way to the net. The rules of the game at this time, allowed a forward to tackle the goalkeeper as soon as he played the ball, and bundle him over the goal line if possible. The back could protect the goalkeeper by holding off the forward with his shoulder and hip, but not with his hands. In these situations, referees found it difficult to know what was really going on in and around the square as the ball dropped in, with the result that they usually let it sort itself out. Tom Ryan was like an octopus and would create all kinds of difficulties for goalkeepers and backs alike. This goal from Jim Morrissey's line ball was one of the many scores that Tom was responsible for, without ever touching the ball.

The Wexford backs took complete control of the game in the second half - Bobby Rackard found his feet and was back to his brilliant best. In the forwards, Dominic Hearn scored a goal, and in five glorious minutes Tim Flood scored two goals and a point. The game was as good as over. From then until the final whistle, it was exhibition stuff, with the Wexford supporters going wild. It was a most humiliating day for Kilkenny hurling, and their fans were heading for home long before the game ended. It was hard to believe that a team like Kilkenny could score only one point in the second half, and that from a free. The final score, Wexford 5-11, Kilkenny 0-07.

Just as in Thurles when we beat Tipperary in 1951, I looked back at the scoreboard several times as I left Croke Park that evening. Again, it was unbelievable! Winning an all-Ireland seemed more than possible now, but it seemed unlikely that I would be part of it. This was the first game in almost four years that I had watched from a seat in the stand. I had now seen the team from a different perspective, and they looked awesome, so sporting and honest that you felt proud to be a Wexford man. The Central Council had decreed that only twenty-one players were to be included in the official squad to receive trophies, and I was not one of them on this occasion. I had more than enough to occupy my mind at the time, and was very happy for the lads. I felt the team was good enough to go all the way. My family and friends were disappointed I wasn't on the team, but I thought there might be another time.

Dublin had also qualified for the Leinster final, and that sent shock waves through Wexford. The defeat we suffered in 1952 was still a sore point and there was a niggling fear as we made our way to Kilkenny for the match. Phil Shanahan, who had won three All-Ireland medals with Tipperary; Tony Herbert, who had won one with Limerick; and Willie Walsh of Kilkenny, had all declared to play for Dublin this year. This made Dublin a seasoned outfit. Over twenty-eight thousand people packed into Nowlan Park, but one of the papers on Monday said it was a bit disappointing because the Kilkenny folk had chosen to go to the seaside on such a fine day. They had obviously seen enough hurling for one year. Wexford fielded the same team as had annihilated Kilkenny and they looked fit as they pucked a ball around before the game. They had been training harder than ever before and it was showing.

As soon as the referee gave the first blast on his whistle, Tom Ryan was up to his tricks. He ran straight down to the Dublin goal and took up a position beside the goalkeeper, Kevin Matthews. The Dublin fans did not like Tom's tactics and they let him know - those behind the goal began to boo him. It was the first time I heard booing at a hurling match. Even some of the Wexford supporters were not happy with his antics, but for a different reason; they thought he was acting a bit stupid. However, others could see the plan and how it was working. This day, Tom's ploy seemed to be to stand in the goalkeeper's light and not let him see the shots that were coming at him. He never left the edge of the square, and every time someone took a shot at goal, Tom was facing the goalkeeper. In a twenty years' career, Nickey Rackard played some wonderful games and scored spectacular goals, but, in my opinion, this was his greatest hour.

The game had started tamely enough, with Dublin scoring the first point and Nickey getting the second. Tony Herbert put Dublin ahead again. Then, from a puck-out, Wheeler doubled on the ball in the air, Nickey caught it about twenty-five yards out and crashed it to the net - it had not touched the ground from the time Nick O'Donnell pucked it out. Minutes later, Wheeler had the ball in the net again, but the score was disallowed because Tom Ryan mistimed his run and was in the net himself before the ball arrived. Dom Hearn got another point before Tim Flood was fouled in front of the goal, and Nickey blasted the 21 yards free to the net. With twenty minutes gone, the score was Wexford 2-02, Dublin 0-04, much the same as it had been two years before. In the final ten minutes of the first half, Nickey got another goal and a point, to leave the score 3-03 to 0-04.

Bobby Donovan, who had moved to his best position at corner forward, got the first score in the second half when he doubled on a dropping ball and found the net. This was like a signal for an all out attack on the Dublin goal as the backs returned ball after ball to the forwards. I had never seen Nickey Rackard play in any position other than full forward, but I had been told that, when he played at centre field and centre forward for Wexford and Leinster, eleven or twelve years before, he had played a different style of hurling. In this game he reverted to his earlier style, moving away out from the goal and challenging for the ball.

This game was a replica of the game against Kilkenny a couple of weeks before, with Dublin getting only one score in the second half, a goal in the last minute. Nickey's new lifestyle and an operation on his knee had given him a new lease on life. Every Wexford player was dominant in his own position in the second half, and Nickey gave an exhibition of scoring goals, his final tally was five goals, one of which was special, and four points

When doing research for this book, I came across many things I had long forgotten, but this goal I remember as if it had happened only yesterday. From my position on the sideline, I saw every move Nickey made, right in front of my eyes. Remember, he was fourteen and a half stone weight and could move very fast. He came straight across the pitch to pick up a ground ball. In his own inimitable way, with the hurl in both hands, he went very low and was in the act of straightening up with the ball in his hand, when one of the backs came charging into him. As Nickey straightened his back, this fellow was lifted off his feet and landed on the broad of his back. Nickey had not taken two steps when another fellow crashed into him. He, too, went sprawling, with the result that Nickey had time to steady himself and look at the goal. He was about forty yards out from the goal and fifteen yards in from the sideline when he hit a deadly propelled missile of a shot that no one even saw until it hit the back of the net. This one tiny flash of play demonstrated the skill, power and courage of the man. There are still old farmers around Carnew and Bunclody who will tell you how Nickey would go into a shed with a bullock weighing half a ton and, single-handedly give him an injection. With the syringe in his right hand, with his left he would grab the bullock by one horn and bend his head back to his ribs while

Nickey always went low to pick up the ball.

he gave him the jab in the side of the neck.

The final score in that Leinster final was Wexford 8-05, Dublin 1-04, and Nickey set a record score which may never be broken: he scored 5 goals and 4 points in sixty minutes of play in senior competition. In two games, against what was considered good opposition, Wexford scored 13 goals and 16 points, and had just 1 goal and 11 points scored against them. It was very interesting to read the papers on the Monday after this Leinster final and see what sports journalists who, only one month earlier had written Wexford off, had to say now. "It wasn't a match, it was a massacre", was one comment. Someone else marvelled at how Jim English picked up balls as a conjurer picks up cards, and extricated himself from all kinds of difficulties in a manner that would have baffled even Houdini. I think that was a great description of Jim's style.

Eight times the ball had passed Kevin Matthews into the net, but still he was one of Dublin's best players. He was put under severe pressure by the antics of Tom Ryan, so much so that Tom was asked to go a little easier on the goalkeeper in the next game, or we might find ourselves playing with fourteen men. Tom had been given a job to do and he was doing it very well, but there was a thin line between fair and foul, and in the interest of the good name of the team, that line should not be crossed.

There was no doubt that we now had some of the greatest hurlers who ever played the game, but there was a serious problem with teamwork, especially in the forwards. We had three men who could win games with their own individual skill. Tim Flood, Padge Kehoe and Nickey Rackard had been doing it for years at club level where there would be more loopholes in defences, but, in top inter-county competition, more teamwork was needed.

The All-Ireland semi-finals of 1954 were both played in

Croke Park on the same day in August. Cork, the champions for the past two years, played Galway; and Wexford met Antrim. It was generally expected that Antrim would be a weak opposition, but not as weak as they turned out to be. For some reason the Wexford selectors did not play Tom Ryan against them. It may have been that they wanted to keep his unusual tactics under wraps while Galway and Cork were looking on. The game was one-sided and Wexford might have been better without it. The biggest cheer of the day was for Jimmy Langton, when he appeared on the pitch to referee the game. The great Kilkenny forward had not been seen in this capacity before. The final score was, Wexford 12-17, Antrim 2-03. Nickey set a new record for an All-Ireland semi-final, scoring seven goals and seven points, but the whole game was a useless exercise. Cork beat Galway rather easily to set up a final showdown between themselves and Wexford on the first Sunday in September.

Since we played in the All-Ireland final in 1951, there had been an improvement in the standard of living in the country. Almost every household now had a radio, albeit some of them needed a good thump now and again to keep Mícheál O'Hehir coming over loud and clear. More people now had cars, and the quality of public transport had improved, with the result that only the very young and the very old were left at home on big match days. In 1951 two or three special trains left Wexford for the All-Ireland final. On this occasion several trains and every available bus would make the journey; and specially chartered planes would bring hundreds of Wexford exiles from Boston and New York. Some of these people would not have been home since they left the country years before. For them it would be an exciting and emotional trip as they brought their banners and bunting telling us where they had come from.

Getting tickets for the game was not a huge issue, only the

Hogan Stand and the upper deck of the Cusack Stand had seating. The Railway and Canal ends and all under the Cusack Stand were standing areas only, so the crowd just kept packing in until the last one came through the turnstiles. It was a miracle no one was suffocated or trampled on. Some said they didn't get a smoke until the game was over because they couldn't get their cigarettes out of their pockets. Others complained of a crick in the neck because they got turned, with their backs to the field of play, and had to watch the game looking over their shoulders!!

There were six rows of seats inside the railing around the pitch in Croke Park at this time, and people would queue from nine o'clock in the morning to get them. Being close to the sideline and below pitch level, they were great for children. It was not unusual to see numbers of men and women with children in these queues. Another custom at the time was, if you had a boy or girl you could lift over the turnstile, you got them in free of charge. There is a story told of a small man from Enniscorthy town, who I won't name, but he was a barber. He always brought a skull cap in his pocket to the games. When he arrived to the gates of Croke Park, he would put on his cap, turn up the legs of his trousers, and wait until some big fellow he knew came along to lift him over the turnstile. It is said he died a wealthy man!

There were many stories told about priests and how fast they could say Mass on the mornings of big games, but I heard one about this priest in Enniscorthy who had no interest whatsoever in hurling. He was saying first Mass in the cathedral on the morning of the All-Ireland final, and when he got up on the pulpit to say his few words, he saw the place was half empty.

"Where are the men who fill these seats every Sunday morning?" he asked. "I'll tell you where they are. They're on their way to Dublin. And where will these men get Mass this morning? It is my opinion that many of them will get no Mass at all today. But, remember this, no matter what the occasion, God comes first, even before Nickey Rackard."

With that, some wise old crack at the back was heard to say, "But on this occasion, Father, Nickey Rackard is God".

Another story I was told recently - by a man who was at the '54 final. He was fourteen years old at the time and he went to the game with a neighbour who had a Baby Ford car. There were two big men in the front seats, and four boys in the back. They left home at five o'clock in the morning as they wanted to get the best seats on the sideline. All the tyres on the car were very badly worn, so they had three spare wheels in the boot. Twice, they had to change a wheel, and each time instead of putting the punctured wheel back in the boot, they just flung it in over the ditch. They were in the queue outside Croke Park at half past eight and their sandwiches were all gone by ten o'clock. They got their seats all right, but it was a long day and a long journey home on an empty stomach. How times have changed!

Seldom before was there such interest in the country in a sporting event, with everyone except Cork people supporting Wexford. In the three games leading up to the final, Wexford had scored 25 goals and 33 points with only 3 goals and 14 points scored against them. It was difficult for the ordinary Wexford supporter to see how their team could be beaten, but the sports writers were not convinced and made Cork slight favourites. They were the All-Ireland champions and had been for the past two years, and would not give up their title easily; the Cork selectors and mentors, as well as the team, were laden with All-Ireland medals; while Wexford's had practically nothing; Cork had Jim Barry, the most successful trainer and manager in the history of the game, but Wexford did not seem to have a manager - those were the comments in the press in the days preceding the final, but we had heard

1954 Team and Subs

Back row: Kevin Sheehan (trainer), Martin Flood (sub.), Nickey Rackard, Bobby Rackard, Patsy Boggan, (selector at back), Jim Morrissey, Nick O'Donnell, Ted Bolger (sub), Mick O'Hanlon, Dominic Hearn, Nick Bowe (selector), Sean Browne (county chairman). Front row: Tim Russell (sub), Bobby Donovan, Jim English, Art Foley, Padge Kehoe, Ned Wheeler, Paddy Kehoe, Billy Rackard, Seamus Hearne, Tim Flood, John Hearn, (sub). (Tom Ryan has left his position and can be seen behind Nicko's shoulder).

it all before. The teams were:

Wexford:

Art Foley

Billy Rackard   Nick O'Donnell   Mick O'Hanlon

Jim English   Bobby Rackard   Ned Wheeler

Jim Morrissey   Seamus Hearne

Paddy Kehoe   Tim Flood   Padge Kehoe

Tom Ryan   Nickey Rackard   Bobby Donovan

The subs: Ted Bolger, John Hearn, Martin Flood, Dom Hearn and Tim Russell.

Cork:

D. Creedon

J. O'Riordan   J. Lyons   T. O'Shaughnessy

M. Fahy   V. Twomey   D. Hayes

G. Murphy   W. Moore

W.J. Daly   J. Hartnett   C. Ring

J. Clifford   E. Goulding   P. Barry.

Much of what happened in the All-Ireland Final of '54 never registered properly in the memory of those who saw it. It was a wonderful game of hurling, with many great performances by individual players, but Bobby Rackard's display in the last twenty-five minutes overshadowed everything else. Both sets of backs were in complete control for much of the game, with the goalkeepers almost redundant.

Wexford were having the best of the exchanges in the first half and led, 1-03 to 0-5, at the break; but really, there was nothing in it as the second half took shape. Tim Flood had put Wexford two points up, when disaster struck. Christy Ring gathered the ball and was bearing down on the Wexford goal. Nick O'Donnell saw the danger and went to meet Ring just as he was about to hit the ball. Christy got in his shot, but they collided and Nicko suffered a broken collar bone and had to be replaced.

It could be said now that the selectors were at fault

because they had no replacement for Nicko. Billy Wickham, of Cloughbawn, had been the sub for the full-back position and many thought he would have been introduced. But Billy was sitting up in the stand with a few more of us who had been dropped from the panel when the GAA authorities restricted to twenty the number of medals available for the winning team.

Ted Bolger was now put in at wing-back, and New Wheeler went to centre-back. Bobby Rackard, on his own suggestion moved to full-back. Few knew that Bobby had damaged a muscle in his leg three weeks previously in a practice match against Tipperary, and was a doubtful starter up to a few days before the game. His only training was to tap a rubber ball against a wall in Tramore, where, for two weeks he was having treatment in the Hydro-baths. If he was tired, he showed no signs of it when he went in full-back. The final score was Cork 1-9, Wexford 1-6.

After a lifetime of playing for and supporting my club and county, there are many games and situations over which I could become very emotional, but when I think of Bobby's achievement in the final twenty-five minutes of this game, I can find no words to describe my feelings. John D. Hickey, the most respected sports journalist of the time, described his feelings as he left Croke Park:

My regrets about the memorable occasion are that I fear the likes of Rackard's display may never again be seen, and I am sorry that I was not a Wexford man for that hour.

Cork people, too, who saw Bobby play in '54, never forgot him, and whenever I visit Cork, I am often asked about Bobby, and what kind of person he was. They thought there was something private and mysterious about him, which in a way was right. Whatever else he was, he had the ability to push himself to the limits of human endurance in a way very few athletes can. I am not saying he did this in every game, far from it, but when the chips were down and the stakes were high, Bobby could deliver and go the extra mile.

There were some strange comments from the press people in the week after the game. Most of the writers thought Wexford had shot their bolt and would be a great loss to the game. One man's view was that some of this team had been playing inter-county hurling for more than ten years and there were no replacements in the pipeline. Another said, *"This game made Ring the most famous hurler of all time because he had won his eighth All-Ireland medal, but the game belonged to Wexford's Bobby Rackard. Such a display must make him the greatest back the game has known, and it's hard to contemplate human beings pushing themselves further."* "What does the future hold for Wexford?" was asked by another of the press men, and he answered it like this: *"While Ring plays for Cork, it is hard to see them beaten, but don't be surprised if Wexford are back in Croke Park on the first Sunday of September, 1955."*

When the post-mortem on the '54 final was over and the results were analysed, there was evidence of hard luck and poor teamwork. The loss of Nick O'Donnell early in the second half, was a serious setback. Tom Ryan, too, had been injured in the first half and his effectiveness was curtailed. Paddy Kehoe, who was having a good game, was injured towards the end and he, too, was a loss. But these things happen, and unless you have subs for every position, you can do nothing about them. The teamwork, also, was something that could be improved, and everyone realised it after this game. Our best forwards, Nickey Rackard and Tim Flood, each tried to win the game on his own, but it did not work. Billy Rackard, who was having a great game at corner-back, lost concentration for a moment, which allowed Cork to get the goal that made the difference at the end.

My own feelings after this game were of great

disappointment and frustration. I felt I had let someone down, especially Bobby, with whom I had soldiered since we were children, and I vowed, if the chance ever came again, I would be ready.

The question now was, would we get another chance? Were there young talented players in the county, who could fit into the team and play well at this high standard? Only time would tell.

A stock-take showed we had about twenty-two players whose average age was twenty-five, and most of us could have five more years playing at top level. The selectors and mentors, too, had lots of experience as most of them had been involved for the past five years. Dr. Paddy Daly looked after our physical and mental well-being now, and he knew the needs of each one of us very well. John Randall had designed a special hurl for each player, and when it got broken he had an identical replacement. Our travel arrangements were always the same, thanks to our loyal hackney drivers. Even though no one had mentioned the word "retiring", a new feeling of urgency had begun to enter the minds, not alone of the players and those in charge of the team, but also of the supporters all over the country. If we were to win an All-Ireland, another major united effort was needed.

Players never look forward to playing games in wet and windy weather, but you have to take the rough with the smooth and get on with it. The Oireachtas competition began almost immediately after the All-Ireland final; then there were the first games of the National League, with all the travelling in bad weather and the short days. Not something to fancy, but with the friendship, loyalty and honesty in the camp, no one was complaining.

For those unable to hold a permanent place on the team, the League often provided an opportunity for them to get a game and show what they could do if given the chance.

Sometimes a sub would be asked to play in a position where he had never played before; that was a challenge which seldom improved his prospects of a permanent place on the team. I was once put in at full-back to play on Christy Ring for the last twenty minutes of a League match. I'm sometimes asked if I ever played on Christy Ring, and I can boast that I held him scoreless for twenty minutes. What I don't say is that we were playing with a hurricane at our backs, so the ball seldom came past centre field. Still, I don't tell lies.

Wexford travelled to Tuam to play Galway in the semi-final of the Oireachtas Cup competition, late in September '54, and came home winners on the score, Wexford 8-05, Galway 2-06. Billy Wickham played at full-back while Nick O'Donnell was recuperating. Clare had again qualified for the final, so it was to be a repeat of the previous year's decider. It was played on the first Sunday of October and drew a crowd of close on twenty-five thousand, an unbelievable number as it was a miserable wet day. Clare were a much better team this year and, after a great game in which the score was level six times, Jimmie Smith scored a point in the last minute, which left the score 2-08 each.

The names of this Clare team are worth recording because they were a great bunch of players who deserved to win more than they did:

M. Hayes

M. Leahy	D. McInerney	M. Donnellan
N. Deasey	D. O'Grady	T. Fahey

J. Smith   D. Sheedy

M. Nugent	D. Dillon	P. Russell
J. Greene	J. Ryan	P. Greene

The replay was in Croke Park again, on the first Sunday of November. Over twenty-five thousand people were there to watch a rip-roaring game in which there was no place for the faint-hearted. Clare won, 3-06 to 0-12, and it was forecast by the press that Clare were about to take over from Wexford as the potential champions in 1955. Wexford may have been a tired team after a hard year, but this was a good Clare team, and they proved it the following summer when they beat the All-Ireland champions, Cork, and also Tipperary, in the Munster championship.

I remember this game for some good reasons, but also for some things which should never have taken place on a hurling field. Mick Hayes, in goal, was Clare's best man, with O'Grady, Sheedy and Jimmie Smith performing heroics, too. Jim English had the best game of his life at wing-back for Wexford. Four different Clare men tried to subdue him, without success.

I have seen Nickey Rackard absorb some rough treatment in his sporting career and never retaliate, but how he remained cool in this game, I'll never understand. In the dressing-room at half-time, he took off his jersey to reveal three of the ugliest injuries I have ever seen on a player's body after a hurling match. There were two bruises on his back which by now had turned black. They were more than ten inches long and were the result of a full blow from the back of a hurl. He had one more on his side, just above his kidney. These were not just red patches accidentally caused by the flat of a hurl; they were deliberate, violent hits, and were not the work of his immediate opponent.

It's interesting the different reception you get from some of the supporters when you come home after being beaten in a game and that which you get when you win. I remember arriving home at Tim Flood's place after being beaten in this Oireachtas final by Clare and we were feeling tired and sore. It must have been two o'clock on Monday morning when we got out of the car and Tim exclaimed, "Oh jainey, Foley is still up with the sow". Foley, of course, was Kevin Foley, who at that time was one of Cloughbawn's foremost senior hurlers and is now that great character we always see patrolling the sideline whenever a Cloughbawn team is playing. Kevin who was Tim's greatest fan, had volunteered to baby-sit a sow which was about to have her litter of bonhams. Tim and I crossed the yard to where Kevin was sitting on a small stool in a shed, well back from the sow, and he was in a foul mood. "What the hell went wrong with yis today, letting them fellas run rings around yis?". "The best team won" said Tim, adding "sure wasn't the commentary in Irish on the wireless, and you don't understand Irish so what would you know about it". "Even if it was in Chinese" said Kevin "I know you never got a belt at the ball, and what was wrong with the backs? They were letting Jimmy Smyth run in like a fish through water. You'd think if they couldn't stop him going in, someone would get him coming out". With that, Tim said "Good night, lads", and left Kevin and myself to finish the discussion. Kevin climbed out over the gate of the shed and as he looked back he said, "I'm sitting there with that ould hoor of a sow for the last five hours and there she is now with only three boneens. She had four but she stood up and walked on one and killed it, and when I tried to save it she attacked me and only I was quick enough to get one leg over the gate she would have destroyed me too. Look at that", he said, "she tore the whole arse out of me trousers, and I was supposed to be going to a dance in Clonroche tonight." He then turned towards the road and said, "Well, feck 'em all anyway, hurlers, sows and women, I'm going home to go to bed. Good night!"

Making good use of the full panel of players, Wexford had a good run at the beginning of the 1954-'55 National League, winning three important games before the winter break. We beat Waterford in Waterford, 4-10 to 2-05. Art Foley, Jim Morrissey and Ned Wheeler were missing for this game, and yet another new goalie was brought in. Peter Barron, from

Rathnure, was the man to fill the vacancy and he did the job well. Kilkenny were beaten in New Ross, 7-05 to 2-05, before a massive crowd. Our last game of the year was in Croke Park, against Dublin. We beat them, 5-08 to 2-03. Nick O'Donnell was fit again and had an outstanding game. I think most of us played every Sunday for four months, as we had to finish the county championship in between the inter-county matches. There was a renewed confidence in the team as we looked forward to 1955. We felt we were on a roll.

What a change five years had made in the lives of a group of Wexford hurlers! We were household names the length and breadth of Ireland, and yet our only achievements were to win two Leinster championships and the Oireachtas Cup. Press and Radio were giving the team great publicity, and we had no bad exposure, which was great for the morale. Some of the stories and yarns told about those mad and exciting times are worth repeating here.

There is one man who tells me the same story every time he sees me. He was reared about a mile or so outside Enniscorthy, and would have been in his early teens in the mid-fifties. He and his friends used walk into the town every Saturday night and stand outside the cinema in the hope they would see one of the county hurlers going in to the pictures with a girlfriend. He said it was very disappointing if they saw one and he had no girl.

Another old man tells about the day he saw Nickey Rackard at a fair in Enniscorthy. This was long before the livestock marts were built, when farmers took their animals to town to sell them on the street. The cattle fair was held on the Island Road, overlooking the Slaney, from the old bridge and out the road as far as was necessary to accommodate all the stock. The street would be very crowded, with no law or order, just each farmer trying to keep his few cattle together while the dealers and jobbers walked about looking for bargains.

This old man was a sexton in a small church just outside
the town, and in conversation his language sounded like the
Scriptures. Because he was totally against attending a
sporting fixture on the Sabbath Day, he had never been to a
hurling match. One fair day, he was standing on the hump of
the bridge where the railway line passes under the Island
Road, when he saw Nickey. He would tell the story like this.

*I was standing on high ground, looking east, when a great
calmness descended on the multitude. Then it was as if the
Lord had said to Moses, 'Stretch out your hand over this mass
of people and animals, and part them and let the good man
walk through'. I watched in amazement as the people, and
even the dumb animals, moved to either side of the roadway.
It was my first and only time to see a living legend. As he
passed by you could feel his presence.*

There was a story, too, told about three neighbours who
had bought their first cars in 1954, but had no idea how to get
to Croke Park. One of them got a bright idea. He knew a man
who often travelled to Dublin by train, and he thought this
fellow might know how to hail a taxi, so he asked him to go
to the game with him. "But it'll cost a fortune to get taxis for
eighteen people! You'd be mad to do that!" said the fellow.
"Oh, no", said the bright-idea man, "you hire a taxi and tell
the driver you'll give him a few bob extra to drive slowly to
Croke Park, and we can tag along behind". They said it
worked.

A few years ago, I met a neighbour of mine on the road one
summer evening, and we stopped for a chat, as we didn't have
much else to do. She was in her early seventies and had
returned from abroad, where she had spent most of her life.
She left home in the early forties and went to England, where
she became a nurse. She worked with the British forces for
the remainder of the war; and then spent many years

working in Australia and New Zealand, before coming home
to spend her last years where she had spent the first. She
saw very little of her family for all the years she was away,
but her father never failed to send her the local weekly paper
until his death in the sixties. In the fifties he would send her
the *Irish Independent* on the Monday after Wexford had
played an important hurling match.

For an hour or more that evening, I listened as this lady
unravelled the story that had been built in her mind by the
power of the press. It was evident from what she said that
she had read the papers with great interest and care. She
talked about things that I had almost forgotten. She recalled
how bad things were when she left in 1941, and remarked
how times had changed and got better as the years passed.

What really amazed me about this woman was her
knowledge of the Wexford hurlers of the '50s. She had got all
her information from the newspapers sent to her by her
father. She would have known the older members of the
Flood, English and Rackard families before she emigrated,
but how she had stored so much in her mind for forty years,
I'll never understand. I was the first person that she ever
spoke to at length about hurling, she had never seen a
hurling match, but she could remember the names of all the
Wexford team.

She said she always compared the Wexford hurlers with
the great "All-Blacks" rugby players that she got to know
while in New Zealand. She asked me to thank the hurlers for
all the memories. She then looked straight at me and said,
"Fifty years ago, you and I would not sit here and talk like
this". For a moment I didn't grasp what she was talking
about, but then my mind flashed back over the years and I
saw her beautiful fifteen-year-old sister who was the same
age as me. I remembered the times I had gone out of my way
to meet her on this road where we were talking now, and how

we would pass each other and look the other way, not because we wanted to, but because we were told to do so by people who knew no better. You see, we were born into different faiths. Like the song says, "Time Changes Everything"!

The defeat by Cork in the All-Ireland final was a bitter disappointment and the wear and tear of another campaign could be a step too far for the older men. Those close to the team who had seen our games in the League so far, had not lost faith. Over a period of five years, we had played over fifty games in major competitions and not once could you say we were "lucky" when we won a game. I often heard Nickey Rackard say, you make your own luck. I think he meant that by being persistent, things would go your way. And if that is true, our success could not be too far off.

Nickey seldom attended meetings of the hurling club in Rathnure or practised in the local field. But he never failed to attend the Annual General Meeting of the club and I can still remember his contribution to the deliberations in January '55. To the boys and young men of Rathnure, he was more than a sporting hero. He was an object of curiosity and hero-worship, and many of them came to the meeting for no other reason than to get a close-up look at the man who was always referred to as "Nickey". The AGM of the club was always held in the old school house and about twenty boys were packed into the back desks long before the meeting was timed to start. It was the custom at the time that when the Priest or the Inspector from the Department of Education entered the school, everyone stood up immediately. The chairman had just called the meeting to order and was going through the formalities, when the door opened and Nickey came in. Every young lad at the back was on his feet in a flash and, strange as it may seem now, every man stood up too. I never saw Nickey so embarrassed, but it just goes to show the magnitude of his popularity at the time.

When asked to address the meeting, he stood up and went to the top table where the officials of the club were sitting and, as he composed himself, it was evident that he had come prepared to say something that he felt was important. He had some notes which he left down on the table. Picture the scene here now. It's two o'clock in the afternoon on the first Sunday of January; there is ice on every pool of water outside and a blanket of snow covers the Blackstairs Mountain high over the village of Rathnure. There's neither heating nor lighting in the now disused schoolhouse, so it's bitterly cold

The old disused schoolhouse in Rathnure.

inside as well. Most of the men attending this meeting are farmers and farm workers and are wearing their heavy work clothes and boots. Nickey looked as if he had come from a different planet. He wore a tweed jacket and waistcoat and a light coloured riding breeches. He had a silk scarf and leather gloves. His dress may have been different, but when he began to speak, he set everyone there at their ease and you could hear a pin drop while he spoke.

His address went something like this. "It's been twenty years since I left school here, and this club is now twenty two years old. I want to congratulate and thank the men who have brought us to where we are today. There has been great improvement in this parish and in the country in general, and I want to congratulate you on the building of the new school and the new hall which is almost complete. No matter how far you travel from the place where you spent your childhood, or how successful you become, there is always something that will draw you back home. In my case it is always the hurling. From the time I was knee high, I have been dreaming of the day when Wexford would win the All-Ireland. It has been a long hard road, but I believe the time has come. It will be a travesty of justice if we don't win in '55. We have the men now, and we have the determination too. I feel we have paid in advance for our All-Ireland medals, and nothing is going to stop us. We here in Wexford and especially here in Rathnure, are now on the crest of a wave as far as hurling is concerned, but it won't always be like that. There are bound to be times when the club will struggle and find it hard to have fifteen good players, and that is the time when our loyalty to this parish will be tested.

Twelve years ago, I nearly made a terrible mistake and, to this day, I find it hard to talk about it. I was twenty-one years of age and very ambitious. Wexford hurling was at a low ebb and the football prospects did not seem much better. I was at University in Dublin and it was difficult to travel to Wexford because of the war and I had been playing in the Dublin championships. Dublin had won the football All-Ireland in '42 and the hurlers reached the final as well, but were beaten by Cork. There was pressure on me to declare for Dublin; I was offered the chance of winning All-Ireland medals. It was a tremendous bait so when the time came to declare my intentions. I decided, for one year at least, to throw in my lot with Dublin.

"When I got home for my Easter holidays that year, one of the first things I did was to drop in to the Garda barracks in Killanne, for a chat with my good friend, Garda Tom O'Rourke. Tom is a Clare man who had won an All-Ireland hurling medal with Dublin in 1927. In the course of our conversation, which took place on Easter Saturday night, 1943, I told Tom of my decision to play with Dublin. Tom was all against it, and an argument started between us. In the end Tom persuaded me to change my mind. At the time, Easter Sunday was the last day for sending in declaration forms. We got a form somewhere, and I signed it. Tom brought the form to Enniscorthy on Sunday morning and gave it to the Wexford delegates who were travelling to Dublin for the annual Congress. It's impossible to say how much I owe to Tom O'Rourke for persuading me to alter my decision.

"No matter what way you look at it, there is a very deep and basic difference between playing for your own county and playing for any other. The feeling I get every time I put on the Wexford jersey, I could never fully capture were I going out to play for any other county. There is always a particular thrill in playing for your own county and for your own people, and it's the same at club level. You play for the sake of the little village, and no man is greater than the club. Each one of us is a cog in the wheel, so let everyone put their shoulder to the wheel and together we'll achieve great things. With a small bit of luck, there will be five All-Ireland medals in this club by the end of this year, and who would have even dreamed of that ten years ago?"

I believe the spirit of Nickey Rackard is alive and well in Rathnure and in Wexford still. There are four ingredients needed to be a good hurler. You need skill, courage, concentration and dedication. I worry about dedication.

1955

From 14 November, '54, to 13 March, '55, Wexford hurlers played no competitive game, and it was an uneasy time for supporters and players alike. I wouldn't say it was a worrying time, but there is always the fear of the unknown and the hard luck. From the unity in the camp oozed a confidence that, until now, was missing. For the winter months the players and mentors would have had very little contact with each other, but they were now an experienced and confident bunch of men and, deep down, their focus was on the championship and the first Sunday of September.

Looking back to the All-Ireland final and the defeat by Cork, we felt the team didn't get the breaks, and the loss of Nick O'Donnell was the difference between winning and losing. Likewise, the Oireachtas Cup Final against Clare would have been won if a full team had been available and if the players had not been so tired. It's so easy to make excuses, but the team had played well in the three League games at the end of 1954, and we knew we were as good as the best. All we needed in '55 was to have the full panel of players available, and that bit of luck that is so important to win games. The type of work most of the players were doing would keep them physically fit over the winter months, and a break from the games and all the pressure would give them time to think of other things.

It was during this time that I first asked myself, "What are you doing for this team? You are there now for more than five years and you haven't exactly been a lot of help when help was needed most". I had given it five years, but Paddy Kehoe and Nickey Rackard had given it fifteen and were still prepared to give it their all. Surely I was privileged to be part of this great team and it would be wrong of me not to get myself in a fit state to reach my full potential. I knew my biggest failing was lack of stamina. I never doubted my hurling ability. Another problem I'd had from a very young age was varicose veins in both legs and, by now, these had become a serious condition; so much so, that if I was hit with the ball on the leg, it would leave me with a pumping feeling in the veins which was very uncomfortable. On a few occasions I had to leave the field when I got hit on the leg with a hurl. In 1955, the team doctor, Paddy Daly, got me a pair of very thick elastic stockings. These stockings covered my foot, with just the toes and heel out, and went right up to the knee. For the rest of my hurling career, I never even practiced without wearing these stockings, and it was as if I had a new pair of legs.

At 13 stone weight and sometimes less, I often felt I was a bit light for my size. The doctor and myself were discussing this one day, and he told me that, at six-foot-two, I could carry another stone. He then asked me about my appetite and how much I would eat; and there was certainly no problem there. Then he said, "I'll treat you for worms". For a minute I thought he was joking, but he wasn't that kind of man, so I just felt a bit embarrassed. Twice a year I would dose the sheep and cattle for worms, but this was getting a bit personal, I thought. Still, I followed his instructions and took the prescribed medication. In two days the treatment proved a visible success. In the following six months, I put on over a stone in weight and felt much stronger. The average weight of the Wexford team was 13st 2lbs, height was 5ft 11½ins and the age was 27½ years. Overall the players and management team would have had more than five years experience of top class hurling. There could be no excuses now: all that was needed was a small bit of luck.

It was the second Sunday of March when we played our first game in '55, it was a League game in Navan against Meath. Even with an under-strength team, we won easily,

5-06 to 1-06. The last game in our group of the League was against Cork, and this was played at Bellefield, in Enniscorthy, on 27 March. If we could win this game, we were into the final of the League and that was very important because it brought much-needed revenue into the coffers of the County Board. We were reminded of this by the Chairman, Sean Brown, when he told us that the only money Wexford got from the '54 All-Ireland semi-final and final was £460, which looked very small when you think of the 84,000 people who attended the final.

Sean need not have worried, because we beat Cork rather easily that day in a game that, for some reason, never lived up to expectations. Even with Christy Ring and most of the team that had beaten Wexford the year before in the All-Ireland Final, Cork didn't seem to have the stomach for a battle, and Wexford won pulling up, the score, 3-06 to 1-04. There were over 10,000 people in Bellefield that day. Most of them were somewhat disappointed, saying we didn't beat them by half enough, while others said, Cork were just pulling the wool over our eyes for the upcoming year's championship. I think, myself, that the Wexford team had learned to spare a bit for the next game. Up until now, we were giving our all in every game, just to please the supporters.

Tipperary had qualified from their group, and the League Final was fixed for Croke Park on the first day of May. This was just what the Wexford team looked forward to now; Cork, Tipperary and Kilkenny, were the teams that stood between us and final glory. We would never be classed as a great team until we beat these counties in the finals of major competitions. Those were the words of Nickey Rackard, and what Nickey said was agreed by all.

Our aim was that Tipperary would be our first victim, in the League Final, and whoever was in our way on the first

The three Rackards (who missed the League final in 1955), from left: Bobby, Nickey and Billy.

Sunday of September would be the second. These words may never have been written on paper, but they were chiselled in the minds of thirty men who had the responsibility of making them come true.

We had the whole month of April to prepare for this League Final, and there is always a great freshness at this time of year. We'd no hard games for almost six months and everyone had wintered well. I knew there would be competition for two positions on the team; one at wing-back and the other at corner-forward. I felt I would not be in contention for either, but I would work hard and my day might come. After three weeks of the most intensive training the team had ever done, amidst great speculation as to how the team would be placed, tragedy struck. Eight days before the game, Bob Rackard, the father of three of the players, died. To say there was sorrow and confusion would be an understatement. The question on the lips of all in the county, and further afield, was: would the lads play, or would they not play? I believe it was the wish of Mrs. Rackard, their mother, that her sons would not play in the week their father was buried, and all complied with her wishes.

There was great disappointment all over the country, and especially in Wexford; so much so, that the attendance at the game fell from an expected 40,000 to 17,000. To their credit, the selectors did their best to balance the team and stop the gaps. It was impossible to replace men like the Rackards, but the players vowed to make a supreme effort and not to let their loyal supporters down.

The team selected to face Tipperary in the League Final of '54 - '55 was:

                          Art Foley
Billy Wickham   Nick O'Donnell   Mick O'Hanlon
Jim English   Jim Morrissey   Ted Bolger,
            Ned Wheeler   Seamus Hearne
Padge Kehoe   Paddy Kehoe   Tom Dixon
Dom Hearn   Tom Ryan   Tim Flood.

The Tipperary team was:

                        Tony Reddan
Micky Byrne   Michael Maher   John Doyle
Connie Keane   Jimmy Finn   John McGrath
            John Hough   Theo English
Liam Devaney   Pat Stakelum   Gerry Doyle
Seamus Bannon   Larry Keane   Tommy Barrett

Every man gave his best in this great game. Jim Morrissey, in his unfamiliar role at centre-back, was the outstanding player on the field. The display by the men who replaced the Rackards that day was proof that we now had a strong panel of players and all had lots of experience too. It was feared before the game that our backs would get the run around. That's why Jim Morrissey was brought back to play at centre-back. Ted Bolger and Billy Wickham, the men brought in to replace Bobby and Billy Rackard, had outstanding games. It was in the forwards that we struggled. Tim Flood got injured, and, even though he didn't come off, he was badly handicapped.

Tom Ryan was moved into full-forward, to replace Nickey, and was doing capers and causing all kinds of problems for the Tipperary backs - so much so, that Mick Maher lost his cool and got himself put off. Now, Tipperary were a man down in the backs, so they brought Pat Stakelum from his unfamiliar position at centre-forward, where he was getting a lesson from Jim Morrissey, to his old position of centre-back, where he went on to play a blinder. Tom Ryan was still doing capers up front, so he, too, got his marching orders. Ned Wheeler got injured and had to leave the field and I took his place. When the game was over and the dust had settled, it was the opinion of the experts that the Wexford forwards had got so much ball, that, if Nickey Rackard had been playing, Wexford would have won with something to spare. It's a game that was soon forgotten, and we prayed that our luck would change for the championship. The final score was Tipperary 3-05, Wexford 1-05. Wexford came home with their spirits and confidence undiminished.

We had now been beaten in two All-Ireland Finals and three League Finals. With the exception of Galway, in the League Final of '51, it was Tipperary and Cork who had hurt us most. More than ever, there was self-belief and confidence in the squad now, but there was also that fear of the unknown. Experts say you need hunger, well this team and its supporters were now starving - there was a famine in the county for success.

A week or two after the League Final, we went to Templemore to play Tipperary again, in a charity game. Even though most of the panel travelled to the game, the selectors put out a very under-strength team. It could be that they wanted to give everybody a game, but I think there was more to it than that. They now knew what their best team was, but they would keep it to themselves until the start of the championship. For a third time, in the month of May, we played Tipperary, this time on the last Monday of the month. It was the bank-holiday weekend, and the game was in Mitcham Stadium, in London. Again, the selectors confused everyone with the team they put out. Billy Rackard was at centre-forward, I was full-forward and Nickey was on the corner. There was no one saying, "Come on lads, let's win this game", it was just a bit of fun.

There are a few things about this trip that still stick in my mind. I have good reason to remember the state of the pitch. The weather had been very warm and dry for the whole month of May and this left the ground like concrete. Especially along by the sideline where there was no grass, it was dangerous. I was running at speed to try to save a ball from going wide over the end-line and, like an idiot, I threw myself along the ground, full-stretch. From my knee to my hip bone, I took off every bit of skin. When I cooled down and my leg was dry, it was

It was nice to get a plane trip in 1955 - returning from playing in London.

like a very bad burn. It spoiled my whole weekend. There were about 10,000 people at this game and, again, the bulk of them were from Wexford - people who had come over to England to find work in the early '40s and '50s. Many of them travelled long distances from all over Britain, to see this team that they had heard so much about. It was a pity we didn't put on a better show for them, but they seemed happy enough just to see us play.

There must have been hundreds there that I would have known, or at least known some of their family back home. Many of these people had left Ireland over a period of fifteen years and some would never have been back. Whole families left Rathnure in the early '50s and I'm sure it was the same all over the country. Most families of my generation have bad memories of family-members and friends leaving for foreign places because, in many cases, it was forever. Some of those who did go might tell you that because of poverty and hardships they would never want to see the old homeland again; but the vast majority would tell you they didn't belong in Britain.

Recently I went to London to the funeral of a family friend and, after the burial, we were brought to one of the old Irish-Centres for a meal. The people there were all old workmates and friends of the man who had died. Most of them were over seventy years of age and some were pretty shook. One old lad came to where I was sitting and, because he was suffering from Parkinson's disease, I found it difficult to know what he was saying to me and I had to ask him a second time. What he said was, "I saw you hurling in Mitcham Stadium in 1955 and it was one of the best days of my life, to see that great team. I was born in New Ross, but there is not a soul there now who would know me". I didn't know what to say, but I took his hand and said thanks, and thanked God for being a small part of a team that gave so much pleasure to so many people.

From a hurling point of view, the game in Mitcham Stadium was of very little use to the team, but it gave the players and mentors an opportunity to get to know each other in a different environment, and that was good. One thing we did learn was that Mick Morrissey was a serious contender for a place on the team. He got his chance to show what he could do, and he made full use of it.

The serious action of '55 started on 26 June, when we played Westmeath in the semi-final of the Leinster Championship, in Croke Park. As far as I can remember, Westmeath had qualified for the semi-final by beating Offaly and Laois in the preliminary round, so they were going to be no pushover. Kilkenny and Dublin would play in the other semi-final on the same day in Croke Park. Since 1 May, when Tipperary had beaten us in the League Final, we had played three or four games, all of which were just a bit of fun. Players had been played in unfamiliar positions and there was no urgency to win these games, but all that would change now as we set out to win our first championship in forty-five years. There was great speculation as to what the team would be for the game. The selectors at this time were Nickey Rackard, Nick Bowe, Peter Hayes, Tim Russell and Patsy Boggan.

This is the team they selected:

Art Foley

| Billy Rackard | Nick O'Donnell | Mick O'Hanlon |
| Jim English | Bobby Rackard | Ted Bolger |

Jim Morrissey   Seamus Hearne

| Martin Codd | Ned Wheeler | Padge Kehoe |
| Dom Hearn | Nickey Rackard | Tim Flood. |

Padge Kehoe was injured and Harry O'Connor took his place. Mick Morrissey replaced Seamus Hearn during the game. We won the game, but not as easily as many people thought we would. The final score, 5-09 to 3-04, did not do justice to the Westmeath effort. The Wexford forwards didn't play well and drove a lot of bad wides. Still, it was a win, and that was all that mattered. Gone were the days of being the "gallant losers". It was Westmeath who got a standing ovation as they left the park, and that was OK with us. We often got the applause too, but that was all we got. One Dublin-based journalist lamented that Wexford were past it, and needed some young blood; even some of our local scribes thought the team was on a downward slide. Most teams play best when they are underdogs; and this kind of reporting is what makes underdogs.

Kilkenny beat Dublin by four points in the other semi-final. This set up another Leinster Final between Wexford and Kilkenny. Before this final took place, strange things were going on down in Munster. Clare had beaten both Cork and Tipperary and were proving to everyone just what a great team they were. Limerick had beaten a good Waterford team and, under the guidance of Mick Mackey, were making good progress with a very young team. On Sunday, 10 July, Clare and Limerick met in the Munster Final in Limerick. Clare were red hot favourites to win this game, having beaten both Cork and Tipperary, but they had no answer to "Mick Mackey's greyhounds", as this Limerick team was being called. Limerick won the game by ten points and gave a whole new look to the All-Ireland Championship. Now, whoever won Leinster would take on Limerick and, after that, only Galway were left to beat. From a Wexford point of view, things looked a bit easier, but there was still a lot of hurling to be played and a lot of sweat to be lost.

It's strange how some things stick in your mind after such a long time, but when I read about today's players having to ask for better conditions and a little more return for their contribution to the game, I think of an occasion when we felt we were being used and taken advantage of. It was early in

July '55, while we were training for the Leinster Final against Kilkenny. Sean Browne, our County Chairman, informed us that we had again been invited to take part in the Oireachtas Cup competition at the end of the year. Now, this competition had been good for us over the years because it had given us good experience, playing against some of the best teams in the country; but some of us felt we had been good for the Oireachtas Committee too, because it   was benefiting from the competition and our efforts were not being recognised. In the space of five years, we had played eleven Oireachtas games before an estimated one hundred and eighty thousand people. Most of these games were played away from home at the end of the year when the weather was poor and the evenings short. On a few occasions, our only recognition after the game was a cup of tea and a sandwich. We never complained because it was an honour to do what we were doing, but it was never nice to come home hungry.

People often ask me how much training we did and what the training was like. At a County Board meeting in '55, someone proposed that the County Board Members decide how the county team should train, and he suggested that there should be collective training. At this time, the only players living outside the county were Jim English, who was living in Bagnalstown, and Seamus Hearne who, I think, was working and living in Cork. The Chairman, Sean Brown, ruled that the selectors and players would decide how the team would train. It was decided that, up to the Leinster Final, we would train two nights each week. To cut down on travelling, some would train in New Ross, some in Enniscorthy, and some in Wexford. Training would consist of two or three laps of the field and six or eight sprints. The remainder of the evening would be spent hurling. I'm not sure what the other lads did, but I spent the other evenings hurling in Rathnure. Most of our training was done with the club.

When the team to face Kilkenny in the Leinster Final was announced, there was one big surprise. Mick Morrissey was on at left half-back. The worry was, he would be marking Sean Clohessy, Kilkenny's most dangerous forward.

The team was:

Art Foley

Billy Rackard	Nick O'Donnell	Mick O'Hanlon
Jim English	Bobby Rackard	Mick Morrissey

Ned Wheeler   Jim Morrissey

Seamus Hearne	Padge Kehoe	Harry O'Connor
Dom Hearn	Nickey Rackard	Tim Flood

The Kilkenny team:

Dick Dunphy

Jim Hogan	John Maher	Mark Marnell
Paddy Buggy	Willie Walsh	Johnny McGovern

PJ. Garvan   John Sutton

Sean Clohessy	Dick Carroll	J. Murphy
Dick Rockett	Paudie Fitzgerald	Mickie Kelly

With Cork and Tipperary gone from the championship, Wexford people felt this was the game to decide who would be All-Ireland Champions and this put extra pressure on the players. We knew these Kilkenny fellows very well, having played against them many times at club and county level, and were confident that we could beat them; but when you see the Kilkenny jersey in Croke Park, some of that confidence disappears.

The game wasn't a classic, but it was tight and tense. It was a very hot day and the scores were level five times in the hour. A few of the things I remember from this game are worth relating. The first ball Sean Clohessy got, he rounded Mick Morrissey and was heading straight for the goal. Mick O'Hanlon came across and met him, bang on, with a shoulder and hip, as only Mick O'Hanlon could. For the remainder of the game, Mick Morrissey won every ball that came up his side of the field and staked a claim for a permanent place on the team, which he got. Nick O'Donnell, at fullback, gave a display, the like of which had never been seen before and the Kilkenny supporters would cringe every time he cleared the ball as they realised what they had let slip from their fingers. Bobby Rackard who was struggling with the heat at centre back, changed places with Billy. Our forwards kept going for goals when points were there for the taking. The final score was, 2-07 each, and the replay was fixed for the last day of July.

When the team was announced for the replay, there were two changes in the forwards. Tom Ryan was back from suspension to take up his position at corner forward, and a complete unknown was in at half forward. Oliver Gough, a twenty-year-old Kilkenny-born lad, who was playing for Ferns club, got his first start. He had played against St Martin's in the Wexford championship the previous Sunday and, even though he was playing on Jim Morrissey, he gave one of the finest exhibitions of hurling I have ever seen. Those who saw that game agreed with the selectors. The replay was a very different game and the standard of hurling was much better. Tom Ryan was back to his old antics and this upset the Kilkenny backs to the extent that Wexford scored five goals. Some of the Kilkenny lads would have played with or against Tom at club level, but they still didn't know how to handle him. The scores were level at half time, Wexford 3-03 Kilkenny 2-06.

Immediately after half-time, a most bizarre occurrence took place and it was the difference between winning and losing. The weather had been very dry and the ground was rock hard, especially near the goals. In those days, the forwards lined up at centre field for the throw in at the start of the game and again to start the second half. Nickey Rackard got the breaking ball from the throw-in and, thinking that Tom Ryan might be arriving up near the goal, he sent in a high lobbing ball. It looked as if the fullback and the goalie were having a few words at the edge of the square when they saw this ball coming in high. The fullback moved out as if to take the ball, but, instead, decided to leave it to the goalie. The ball dropped on the hard ground between them and bounced over the goalie's head into the empty net. It was the softest goal Nickey ever scored, but a very important one, just the same. The reaction of the Wexford fans was as if someone had just told a very funny joke; I don't think the Kilkenny people saw the joke.

Billy and Bobby Rackard exchanged places after half time, and Billy gave such an exhibition at centre half that he was named "Man of the Match" and got "Sports Star of the Week" also. He became one of the best centre backs of all time as he had more freedom to express himself out the field. Bobby was much tighter in the corner than Billy and developed a great understanding with Jim English in front of him. Kilkenny piled on the pressure in the second half, but could not break through the Wexford backs. On another day, at another time, Kilkenny would win games like this, but not here. The final score of, 5-6 to 3-9, didn't do justice to Wexford's superiority in the game. Kilkenny people would say that only for Nickey's soft goal the result would have been different, but we didn't see it that way, we were just "making our own luck".

The feeling now was that we could forge ahead a bit and then, like a good tug-of-war team, hold our advantage until the opposition got a bit tired, and then we could pull away and win. It is normally a time for rejoicing and great celebrations when we beat Kilkenny in the Leinster championship, but this time the celebrations had to be put on hold because, owing to the drawn game, we had to play Limerick the following Sunday in the All-Ireland semi-final. Again, this game would be in Croke Park; it was going to be an expensive time for Wexford supporters, but no one was complaining.

There was only one week for the pressmen and the pundits to give their opinion on how the game against Limerick would go and there were some wild statements made. It is a fact that, on average, the Wexford team were five years per man older than Limerick, so it would seem that Limerick would have an advantage in speed. It was argued too, that Limerick had the greatest player and tactician of all time as their manager - Mick Mackey. What was worrying the Wexford players was, would we have fully recovered from such a strenuous game the previous Sunday? We knew very little about this Limerick team, only what we were reading in the papers. They had three weeks rest since the Munster final; we had just one, but we weren't worried, it could work either way. Our team was much bigger and heavier and we had an advantage in experience. When it was announced, a few days before the game, that the 33 year old Paddy Kehoe would replace the 20 year-old Oliver Gough in the Wexford half forward line, the Dublin press said that Wexford were over confident. When Wexford and Limerick had met in the All-Ireland Final in 1918, Limerick won, 9-05 to 1-03.

After another week of scorching sun, Croke Park was like a bake house and over fifty thousand spectators congregated to see this unusual pairing in an All-Ireland semi-final. The attendance was a new record as the previous best was thirty-nine thousand. Wexford were still a huge draw, and the GAA was laughing all the way to the bank once more.

The Limerick team were first on the pitch. It was the first time we saw a team race from the dressing room making swipes and swishes as if they were being attacked by a swarm of bees. It was in stark contrast to the way Wexford made their appearance. Our lads always looked like they were there to do a day's work. I can still see Mick O'Hanlon that day as he strolled out on the pitch. You would think he was going for the cows. Limerick got a great reception when they appeared, but it was nothing to the Wexford roar that greeted the Wexford team.

The game started quiet enough, with the Limerick lads looking a bit nervous. Nickey Rackard scored a point and then Jim English sent over a long range point, to give Wexford an early lead. Against the run of play, Limerick scored a goal; this gave them a lift and we began to see some of the speed and skill that had surprised every team in Munster. They put Wexford under a lot of pressure for the remainder of the half, and were ahead at half time, 2-02 to 1-03. Nickey Rackard was very unhappy with the first half display of the team and let everyone know in no uncertain terms before going out for the second half. I remember one thing he said was, "Half of this Limerick team are like schoolboys and if they beat us we are disgraced forever".

Nickey always led from the front, and this time it was no different. The first ball he got after the restart, he took on his marker and made some ground before passing it out to Paddy Kehoe who put it in the back of the Limerick net. The speedy Limerick forwards could make no progress against our backs in the second half. Padge Kehoe sent over two or three points, before Dermot Kelly scored Limerick's only score in the second half, a point. It was hard to believe that this team, who had won the Munster Championship, could get no score in the last twenty-five minutes of this game. Wexford won, 2-12 to 2-03. Billy Rackard sent over a point from a free that day, from all of ninety yards. It might not look a great achievement with the ball that is used in today's game, but the ball was that bit heavier then, and to score from seventy yards would be near the limit.

The only prize for winning a semi-final is a place in the final and, even though you have nothing to show for it, it's a wonderful feeling. Only Galway stood between us and our All-Ireland medals now, but we had bad memories of playing Galway in finals. They beat us in the League Final in '51, which was a great disappointment to us as we missed out on a trip to America, and they beat us in the Oireachtas Finals of '50 and '53. So we were not over-confident going into this final. Nevertheless, every member of the team was playing better than ever before, and the whole county were preparing for victory. The support of the neutrals was now split down the middle because they felt Galway deserved to win an All-Ireland too.

Never before were there such preparations for an occasion in County Wexford as there were for this final. Johnny Coady, the local tailor in Rathnure, had to get help from outside the county to contend with the number of new suits needed for the first Sunday of September. Fellows who never wore a tie bought new neckties for the occasion. Women had new dresses made, and many got their first perm. Once again, only the children and the old people would be left at home, so the radio would be set on Radio Eireann with the batteries fully charged.

It was while training for this final that I first heard the word 'tactics' mentioned. Often two or three players would have a chat about some plan that might improve their game, but never a "game plan" made by the players and management collectively. On one occasion, after a short discussion, someone said, "What's wrong with the tactics we are using, any way? Sure, aren't we winning games, so why change them?" With that, Nickey said, "Get the ball up in front of the goal as quick as you can and we'll take it from there". I often ask myself, what did this team have that made it so complete? And the only answer I can come up with is that we had played so many games together, we had a wonderful understanding of each other's style. Most of us had been together for five years by '55 and had played over one hundred serious games. We were big and very strong under the dropping ball, and this upset many a good ball player. We had courage and a good temperament and our first touch was near perfect.

There was great attention to detail now, and nothing was left to chance. Dr Daly attended to the needs of each player, both physically and mentally. He knew the circumstances of the private life of each individual, and was meticulous in his work to have everyone happy and relaxed for the big occasion. Like Nickey Rackard, Dr Daly was an alcoholic and it was a great credit to both men that they gave up the drink for a few years, in the interest of this team. What a tragedy it was that they both went back to their old ways and destroyed their own lives and the lives of those who loved them, but that's another story!

John Randall, who made our hurls, was a master craftsman and he, too, must get great credit for his part in our success. John had three different stamps for his hurls: one hurl was stamped with the words, "Randall, Hurley House, Killurin", on another were the words "Randall Special", but on the ones he made for the county players, he put no stamp until the player said, that's exactly what I want; then he had a special stamp which read, "Randall Special, Hurley House, Killurin, Co Wexford". All Randall hurls were made by hand as there were no machines for hurl making then. It was a skilful, but tedious job, making these special hurls and, unless you had the proper piece of ash, it could not be done. Making these specials must have cost John a fortune in time alone; he used to work on them at night time, when he would have the workshop to himself, and it was fascinating to watch him at work. One night I called and he showed me ten or twelve hurls he had made for the different players; I couldn't believe the contrasting style.

John would say, mishandling the ball once could lose a game; and how right he was! Little things add up to something big.

There's a number of things you can make sure are right, long before you take the field, your gear for instance. On three occasions in five years we had changed the type of jersey we wore and had also discovered that a wide elastic band is much more comfortable in your shorts than a narrow one. The quality of our socks was much improved too, but there was still great concern about the quality of boots available. Through some business contacts, Billy Rackard discovered that a lightweight boot of very good quality could be made to measure. These boots would be costly, but Billy, being the good businessman that he is, got the go ahead from the County Board and had a rep. from this manufacturer measure our feet one evening after training. As there were no showers in Bellefield at that time, the rep. had a rather unpleasant job! The boots were very light. The uppers were made of very soft leather and came up around our ankles. The soles were of very good quality leather, with aluminium cogs. The cogs could be moved to where they were most comfortable. It was unbelievable, the difference these boots made.

The training for the All-Ireland went well, with no injuries. We played Kilkenny in New Ross, on the 24 August, in a game that was classed as a dress rehearsal for the final. It was the kind of game that usually ends in a draw. Everyone got a run, and all made sure that no one got hurt. Kevin Sheehan of Enniscorthy was the official trainer of the team and Sid Bluett, a Kilkenny man, was masseur. These men got very little publicity back then. There was a church-gate collection for the training fund on the Sunday before the game, and a sample figure of the kind of money collected was: Enniscorthy £71, Wexford Town £53 and Bunclody £33.

Galway came into this final at a great disadvantage.

Wexford had played four games to reach the final and all these games were played in Croke Park. Galway had got a bye, straight into the final. Wexford were playing well and had the results to prove it, so we were justifiably confident. Galway, on the other hand, came in from the dark with nothing done to show their form. Wexford fielded the same team as had beaten Limerick, with just one positional switch. Ned Wheeler went centre forward and Padge Kehoe was back on the wing.

The team that won the All-Ireland Championship for Wexford after a lapse of forty five years was:

Art Foley

Bobby Rackard	Nick O'Donnell	Mick O'Hanlon
Jim English	Billy Rackard	Mick Morrissey

Jim Morrissey   Seamus Hearne

Paddy Kehoe	Ned Wheeler	Padge Kehoe
Tom Ryan	Nickey Rackard	Tim Flood

The Galway Team:

T. Boland

J. Fives	B. Power	W. O'Neill
M. Burke	J. Molloy	T. Kelly

J. Salmon   W. Duffy

J. Duggan	J. Young	P. Duggan
P. Egan	J. Burke	T. Sweeney

The travel arrangements for the Wexford team and mentors on the first Sunday of September '55, were the same as they had been for the past five years. One car would bring the Wexford District members, one car the Horeswood and New Ross men, two cars would bring the Enniscorthy lads and our faithful driver, Martin O'Dwyer from Ballywilliam, would bring Billy Wickham, Tim Flood, Bobby Rackard, Jim English and myself. On our trips to Croke Park, we always left home about half nine in the morning and would arrive at our hotel, beside the Phoenix Park, at about twelve thirty. We

ALL-IRELAND WINNING TEAM 1955

Back row: Kevin Sheehan (trainer), Padge Kehoe, Jim Morrissey, Martin Codd, Nickey Rackard, Tom Ryan, Ted Bolger, Nick Bowe (selector), Oliver Gough, Billy Wickham, Mick O'Hanlon, Tom Dixon, Harry O'Connor, Dr. Paddy Daley, Ned Wheeler, Billy Kielty. Front row: Tim Russell (selector), Tim Flood, Bobby Rackard, Jim English, Paddy Kehoe, Mick Morrissey, Nick O'Donnell, captain, Art Foley, Chris Casey, Billy Rackard, Dom Hearn, Seamus Hearne, Sid Bluett (masseur), Peter Hayes (selector).

would have a cup of tea and ham sandwiches and then go for a bit of a stroll before we went to Croke Park. That was our routine for years and we never saw a reason to change it. We thought it best to sleep in our own beds on the night before a game.

The Wexford team were very relaxed in the dressing room before this game, and, as it was a third final for most of us, we knew what the atmosphere would be like when we'd go out on the pitch. It can be the most terrifying time for those who have not experienced it before. There were many seasoned Wexford hurling people who were lamenting that it wasn't Cork or Tipperary we were playing in this final because they had a feeling we could beat them all now. The more cautious supporter was saying, we'll take this one now because we have earned it, and perhaps next year we'll meet one of the big boys in the final. The players knew they had one hour to beat Galway and then we could think about next year.

Seventy eight thousand people were in Croke Park for the game and, as always, Wexford fans were in the majority. They didn't have to wait long for the action to start as, after just two minutes, Nickey Rackard took every one by surprise when he lashed on a ground ball, and Wexford were a goal up. Tim Flood got a point then, and the Wexford followers were making themselves heard in no uncertain way until Paddy Egan scored a goal for Galway. Joe Salmon, who was Galway's best player in the first half, sent in another ball to eighteen year old Egan and Galway were in front when he lashed it to the net again. Galway were putting on a lot of pressure coming up to half time, but our backs were holding well and Wheeler scored our second goal just before half time, leaving us two points behind at the break.

One thing I remember well about that first half was Seamus Hearn's effort to stop Joe Salmon. Joe was one of the most stylish players I ever saw, and he was very fast too. Seamus had this never-say-die attitude and he stuck in behind Salmon and hooked him again and again. Seamus had a unique way of hooking. He held the hurl in both hands and, with an upward jerk, he would almost pull the hurl from your hands. There is nothing so frustrating, or as tiring, as to have someone continually hooking you. And it told on Joe Salmon in the second half when Seamus was out in front and gave a man-of-the-match display. Wexford would have a slight breeze in their back in the second half, but still there was some concern in the dressing room. The forwards had a good supply of the ball, but were not scoring enough. The backs gave away two early goals, but had settled down well. Nickey looked worried enough when he said, "Come on lads, we have only half an hour to do this".

The second half was on for almost ten minutes when Seamus Hearne got the first point. Padge Kehoe got the equaliser and then Nickey, Tom Ryan and Nickey once more, put us three points up, and we went cruising. Galway got a point from a free. A great Wexford move saw Tim Flood finish to the net. Ned Wheeler got two points. Padge, Tim Flood and Jim Morrissey all scored points, before Joe Salmon got Galway's only score from play in the second half. Even with Wexford eight points ahead, with the score, 3 - 13 to 2 - 08, the relief I felt at the sound of the final whistle is something I'll never forget.

You will never know what you will do at a time like this, until it happens. It affects different people in different ways. Young people shout and laugh, while old people cry and thank God that they have lived to see this day. I saw people running that day, scarcely knowing what they were doing, and others just standing where they were, crying. From the subs bench we raced onto the pitch to congratulate the men who had made it all happen, but we just got lost in the thousands who were there before us. It seemed an age before we got across the park to where the cup would be presented to Nick O'Donnell. Nicko was a man of few words, and he didn't keep us there too long.

I found myself isolated, away from any other member of the panel, as I turned to go back across the pitch to the dressing room. People whom I had never seen before put their arms around me or shook my hand as if I had done something to win the game. More than anything else now, I wanted to see Nickey Rackard. On my way back to the dressing room, I met the odd person I knew and stopped for a word. When I mentioned Nickey to one of these, he said, "Nickey is gone in long ago". This surprised me, as I thought Nickey would never get away from this crowd. When I got into the dressing room, Nickey was sitting down with his elbows resting on his knees and his head in his hands. I made my way across to shake his hand, when he stood up and with a far away look on his face kept saying "Unbelievable! Unbelievable!"

Nickey was a big man in every sense of the word and had an unquenchable zest for life. He wanted to live life to the full and this brought him to the brink at times. He liked all kinds of sport, but his love and passion for hurling ruled above everything else. All his life he had dreamed of winning an All-Ireland medal, and twice his dream had been shattered in Croke Park on Final Day. He had played in fifteen championships, most of the time when the team were "no hopers", but he followed his dream and now it had just come true. He was in total shock and could not believe the long wait was over. I think he was sorry in a way that it had to be Galway that we had beaten as their only championship match had ended in defeat. It would be much sweeter to beat one of the aristocrats of Munster.

I had often wondered what it would be like to come home

to Wexford and Rathnure if we ever won an All-Ireland Final, but not in my wildest dreams did I imagine the real thing. I can't think of anything else that would make so many people so happy. There were nights and weeks of receptions and celebrations, most of which I have forgotten years ago, but a few still are fresh in my memory. The reception for the team after the match was in the International Hotel in Bray, on the night of the game, and what I remember most about that night was the massive crowd that converged on the place. By eleven o'clock that night the doors of the hotel were locked and to say the place was full would be wrong. It was jam-packed from top to bottom. Every space on the ground floor was full and all the stairs and bedrooms were stuffed with people. It was crazy, but no one cared.

I remember waking in the morning and thinking, I'll go out and get a paper. It was about ten o'clock and there were still people asleep all over the place in the hotel. When I went out on the road there were more people asleep in cars and in gardens. Some of the revellers who were in the hotel had thrown pillows and blankets out through the windows to their friends who could not gain admittance. I walked down to the seafront and, as I walked past a bit of waste ground near the railway station, this fellow popped his head up from the grass and weeds and asked, "What time is it?" I said, it must be ten o'clock. "Jasus", he said, "it's not! I have to be at work in Donohoe's at nine o'clock". "Don't worry", I said, "There'll be nobody working in Enniscorthy this morning at nine o'clock!"

The journey home to Wexford on Monday evening was slow and emotional. The people of Wicklow were out to greet the team in every village and at every crossroads, and this was greatly appreciated; but the feeling of joy and satisfaction as we approached the border of our own county was indescribable. There was a huge bonfire just inside the border and hundreds of very excited people. For five years these people had hoped and prayed that this day would come, and they had never lost patience. It is difficult to put into words one's feelings and thoughts at a time like this, but my greatest memories would be: first the sound of the final whistle on the day of the game, and second would be the sheer joy and pleasure in the eyes of the genuine hurling people who were there in their thousands that evening on the road home to Wexford. It was almost impossible to get into Gorey and, by the time we got back on the road again, we were an hour and a half behind schedule. Carloads of people had come to meet the team, and this caused all kinds of confusion on the road. When these people discovered that they could make very little progress, they turned back, with the result you had hundreds of cars on the road in front of the team before we got near Enniscorthy. The town was bursting at the seams with people from all over the county, as well as those who had come in from Carlow and Kilkenny to celebrate.

The fear of someone being injured is what I remember best from that night in Enniscorthy. When we did eventually reach the town, we climbed onto the back of a lorry on the Island Road to be driven through the streets up to the Duffry Gate where there was a reception platform. A number of men caught hands and surrounded the lorry as it moved slowly through the crowd. I don't think those fellows enjoyed that part of the celebrations. It was scary, to say the least. As I try to think back to all the celebrations, all the functions, all the dinners, all the receptions and all the speeches, I can remember very little, but one thing I do remember well is Sean Brown's opening line to every speech he made. Sean was chairman of the County Board in Wexford and was invited to speak at all functions to celebrate the team's victory. His opening line to every speech was, "I'll be very brief", but, being a professional politician, Sean never was brief.

The Wexford hurlers' first appearance, as All-Ireland Champions, was in a game against Tipperary, played in Rathnure on 18 September, '55. This game was in conjunction with the opening of the new "John Kelly Memorial Hall" in the village. To most of Wexford's "adoring fans", this was just a fun game and another day of celebration, but to the people of Rathnure, and especially to Nickey Rackard, it was much more. The new hall was named after John Kelly, who was one of the great leaders of the 1798 rebellion in Wexford, and who, according to folklore, was born and reared in the same house as Nickey. I always had the feeling that Nickey modelled himself on John Kelly; he, too, was big, strong and fearless, and would die for the cause.

The field where this game was played was part of the farm where Nickey and his Rathnure team-mates had developed their skills while at school. It was nineteen years since he left school, and only once, in 1940, do I remember him playing a game in his native parish. It was here that the dream started, and he could yet scarcely believe it had all come true.

Some of the founding members of Rathnure G.A.A. Club with Nickey Rackard, from left: Pat Byrne, Nickey Rackard, Tommy Colclough, Mike Mooney, Mickey Redmond and James Brennan.

For the people of Rathnure too, and especially for the older men who had nurtured and promoted the game in the parish, this was a great occasion. One third of the team who would line out against Tipperary, had learned their hurling here at the foot of the Blackstairs Mountains.

For the six founding members of the Rathnure hurling club who had entered their first Junior team in the championship in 1932, and were present, it was a great occasion. To make such progress in twenty-three years was a great achievement. The story is told how these six men were sitting around the table at the first meeting of the club, when the question of the entry fee for their team come up. This fee was something like two shillings and six pence, in old money. Now, most of these men were small farmers, and, it being the start of the economic war, money was scarce, very scarce; so there was a problem. They sat there looking at each other until one put his hand in his pocket, took out a ten shilling note, put it on the table in front of the newly appointed treasurer and said, "That'll see us through the first year". This man was Nick Mernagh, the local shopkeeper. How times have changed! One hundred and thirty thousand Euros is what it took to run the same club in 2004.

The great fear in Rathnure, in the week before the game, was that we would not be able to deal with the number of people we knew would arrive for the game. Someone got the idea to put square bales of straw all around the pitch, so that two rows of people could sit down, and the remainder could look in over the top. It worked, and six thousand happy spectators saw the game. The Wexford lads played with a smile on their faces and won 7-15 to 3-06.

All through the winter of '55 - '56, the celebrations continued, with the All-Ireland cup being brought to every parish in the county. There was no rest for the players as every fixture had to be fulfilled. The first competitive game for the new champions was the semi-final of the Oireachtas Cup, against Clare, to be played in Limerick on the first Sunday of October. This was a new experience for our supporters and thousands of them indicated their desire to make the trip, so special trains were put on to take them there. It was also a chance for Clare to prove to their supporters that their defeat of both Tipperary and Cork in the championship, was no flash in the pan. The press, too, were hinting that Clare would win this game, and I remember the Wexford lads reading the papers that morning and laughing at the idea. It was there for all to see now, the whole team was bubbling with confidence. It was as if a great weight had been lifted from our shoulders. It took five years to crawl to the top and we intended staying there for a while. Clare, too, had a huge following in Limerick that day, and they were very noisy in the first half as their team tried to bully Wexford into submission. These were the wrong tactics, and we pulled away in the second half and won the game, 5-07 to 1-09.

Three things I can still remember from that trip to Limerick. First was Billy Rackard's performance in the game. I have seem Billy play many, many, great games, but this one I remember best. He was majestic. My second memory is the huge number of women and children who were looking for autographs outside the Wexford dressing room. This was a new experience for the players. My third memory had nothing to do with hurling. We had travelled to Limerick on the Saturday evening before the game and, after getting a meal, a few of us made our way to the function-room in the hotel where we were staying. There were two or three musicians, and just a handful of people sitting about. I noticed this fellow with a northern accent, and plenty of beer in him, begging the M.C. to let him sing a song. Eventually the lads in the band gave him a hand up. He stood with one arm around a pillar on the corner of the bandstand and, with a bit of backing from the man with the piano accordion, he sang "The Green Glens of Antrim". You could hear a pin drop while he was singing, and, when he finished, he got a standing ovation from the few who were there. With everyone shouting for more, he slowly got down from the stage and left the room in tears. He had one of the finest singing voices I have ever heard, but he must have had a problem too.

On 16 October, we were back in Croke Park to play Dublin in the League, and won, 5-08 to 4-05. One week later we were in Croke Park again, for the Oireachtas Cup final against Kilkenny. These games with Kilkenny were always special. We had beaten them in the championship by just one goal, after a replay, and that was one of the reasons why over thirty thousand people were in Croke Park for this game. The Dublin press agreed that the game was a classic and, by far, the best game played in '55. Wexford won, with the score 3-11 to 3-04. The real value of all these games was that the full panel of twenty players was getting games and gaining experience, and this would pay off in the year ahead. The following Sunday, we played a League game against Waterford in Wexford Park and won, 3-08 to 2-03.

From a financial point of view, we knew that the League was very important to the County Board, but I don't think that was what drove us on. It was the supporters who had followed us through thick and thin, and who were now reaping their reward. We had reached the stage where the whole country expected us to win no matter who the opposition was, and that was a great feeling, but a big responsibility too. On 9 November, which was one week after the Waterford game, Rathnure and Enniscorthy St Aidan's were to play the Wexford county final in New Ross. There were thirteen of the county panel involved in this game, so, to say the least, it would be interesting. I don't think people outside the two clubs involved were too worried about who would win this final, but St Aidan's had won the three previous years, so perhaps the neutral was on Rathnure's side.

The day was misty and wet, but a record crowd saw a dour, but exciting, game. The players knew each other's style so well, it was a game of cat and mouse, with the side-line mentors playing a vital role. Rathnure played Nickey Rackard at centre forward, to keep him away from Nick O'Donnell, and played a man by the name of Tom Murphy, who was a strong physical type of hurler, on Nicko to try keep him quiet. It worked on the day, and was one of the reasons Rathnure won, 2 - 9 to 2 - 5.

On the following Sunday, a tired and weary Wexford team went to Kilkenny to play their last League game of '55, against the home team. It was the fifth meeting of these rivals in competitive games in less then a year and, for a second time, the game ended in a draw. We now had more then two months to rest and look back on what had been, up to now, the most successful year in the history of Wexford hurling. We looked forward to '56 with confidence. We had come through a tough and tiring year without injury or harm, and that was a bonus.

All of Wexford had now gone hurling mad, with the result that goal posts were appearing in fields near villages and at crossroads all over the county. From Hook Head up to the Wicklow border and beyond, and from the dunes at Curracloe across to the Blackstairs Mountains, men and boys were trying to become hurlers overnight. This was great for some, but a few were not so lucky. I knew two grown men who broke legs trying to play hurling on very uneven ground, and another who, from sheer awkwardness, lost an eye.

When a few fine days would come in springtime in the mid '50s, my neighbour would lend me his tractor to work at night, to speed up the tilling. The tractor was taking over from the horse on the land, and men like my father, who had worked with horses all their lives, were being made redundant. My father never agreed to buy a tractor, and worked the horses every day until his death in 1960. He was 77 years of age and cared for and loved his horses. It's an old saying that it's an ill-wind that blows nobody good, and so it was with the disappearance of the horse from the farms of Ireland. In '55, 18,000 working horses from the farms of Ireland, were exported to Belgium for the horse-meat trade.

A new kind of horse-dealer had appeared on the scene. These men were from the travelling community and saw a chance to make a few pounds. One of them I got to know very well because he was a great follower of the Wexford hurling team. Born on the side of the road in a tent, he could neither read nor write. In a few years he became one of the new rich, and bought a house and a bit of land and settled in the community. He was one of the first travellers to purchase a van and, for the summer months, he would go back on the roads, but he always appeared in Croke Park to support Wexford on the big days. He once offered me two hundred pounds which, he said, was only a fraction of the amount he had won in a bet with his friends from County Cork.

The winter of '55 - '56 passed very quickly. The McCarthy Cup had been to every parish in County Wexford, and there was great speculation as to where it would be in one year's time. Not once did I hear a supporter say he or she had seen enough and was satisfied. It is never like that, and people always want to see more and more of a good thing. The players' view was that they had spent years trying to reach the top of the mountain and they were in no hurry to go back down again. We had won one All-Ireland, and that was great but the feeling was that we had been lucky. We had beaten Kilkenny by one lucky goal, and avoided Cork and Tipperary.

Between them, Cork and Tipperary had won the previous six All-Irelands, and people from those counties would tell us we were lucky. That kind of talk hurt a bit, but they had a point and we accepted that, but we hoped there would be another day at another time.

Not a ball had yet been hit in '56 when the players and officials were laying out their stall for the coming year. The County Board Officials and the Selection Committee of '55 were all returned to office for '56. The finances of the County Board were in good shape, thanks to our good run in the League, so everyone was happy. The only new player brought into the panel, in '56, was a young goalkeeper by the name of Pat Nolan, from Oylegate. After years of searching, the selectors had found a man who was capable of stepping into Art Foley's boots at any time. When Art later emigrated to America, Pat Nolan took his place in goal and had a long and brilliant career, winning two All-Ireland medals.

1956

Our first public appearance in '56, was in Ferns on the last Sunday of January, to play a charity game against Dublin. We would play several games like this over the next few months, with huge crowds turning up every time. We had a panel of about twenty two players now and the selectors were happy and confident that these men could do the business in a never-to-be-forgotten year. There would be no collective training until the evenings got long. We would play a game every Sunday and each player would get a run. If a player had a slight injury or some other problem, he was excused. There was no pressure put on anyone. Each player was responsible for his own first touch and this, I believe, helped them to become a great team. We would get in a bit of ball practice at every opportunity. The ball-alley and the gable end of the house were used for practice, and those lads who had a day or a half day off work, would make use of the daylight hours.

Our first big test was in Wexford Park against Cork, in a League game, on 12 February. If we could win this game, we were into the League final and this would be of great financial benefit to the County Board and, indirectly, to the hurling team. There were great preparations in Wexford town for this game as a record crowd was expected. Even the publicans got in on the act and got permission to open from one to two o'clock in the afternoon and from five to eight o'clock in the evening. Never before did so many people watch a game of hurling in County Wexford, but the game itself was a bit of a disappointment. Wexford played steadily in the first half and pulled away in the second half to win by six points.

The Wexford Team was:

Art Foley

Bobby Rackard   Nick O'Donnell   Mick O' Hanlon

Jim English   Billy Rackard   Mick Morrissey

Jim Morrissey   Seamus Hearne

Paddy Kehoe   Martin Codd   Padge Kehoe

Tom Ryan   Nickey Rackard   Tim Flood

The League Final would not be played until May and we didn't yet know who would be in the final with us. We did no heavy training for the next three months, but played games almost every Sunday. Six Wexford men were selected on the Ireland Team to play the Combined Universities in February. Bobby Rackard, Nick O'Donnell, Billy Rackard, Jim English, Jim Morrissey and Tim Flood were selected, while Nickey Rackard was captain, and full forward, on the Universities team. With Jim English captain of the Ireland team, it meant both captains were from Rathnure, which was a great honour for the club. We went to Limerick to play the home team, in a challenge game for charity, on the last Sunday of February.

In early March, Leinster beat Connacht in the semi-final of the Railway Cup and qualified for the final against Munster on St Patrick's Day. This game against Connacht was played in Ballinasloe, which was another long journey, in bad weather, for the players. The Railway Cup Finals of '56 brought almost fifty thousand fans to Croke Park. Munster and Ulster were in the Football Final, but it was the hurling game that was the big draw. With ten of their team involved, Wexford supporters were there in their thousands and each one confident that their team would sweep all before them this year. The Dublin pressmen were not so confident that Leinster could beat the might of Munster. They were saying how Munster had won twenty-two inter-provincial titles since the competition began, and Leinster had won only six. Between them, the Munster men had over thirty All-Ireland medals, while the Leinster men had only ten. In the previous fifteen years, Leinster had won only one title. Those were the kind of headlines we were reading in the papers.

The Leinster team was:

Art Foley

| Bobby Rackard | Nick O'Donnell | Des Ferguson |
| Jim English | Billy Rackard | Willie Walsh |

Jim Morrissey   Christy O'Brien

| Sean Clohessy | Ned Wheeler | Tim Flood |
| Liam Cashin | Nickey Rackard | Dick Rocket |

Seamus Hearne was in the subs.

The Munster team was

T. Reddin

| M. Byrne | J. Lyons | T. Shaughnessy |
| V. Twomey | J. Finn | J. Doyle |

P. Stakelum   J. O'Connor

| J. Carney | D. Kelly | J. Smith |
| S. Power | J. Hartnett | C. Ring |

Leinster won this game with the score, 5-11 to 1-07, but it was the manner in which they went about their work and how some individuals seemed to take the opportunity to display their talents, that made it a very special day for those who appreciate the skills of hurling and were lucky enough to be there. Tim Flood, who was now at the pinnacle of his career, played that day as if he was just there for the fun of the game. After the first ten minutes it was obvious who was going to win, so we just sat back and enjoyed it. I saw Tim that day as I had so often seen him in the farmyards around home on thrashing days when he was a teenager. He would never be quiet, especially at dinner break. If there were children there, he would set them wild and have them "fighting". If there were no children, he would start playing tricks on the old lads, and I saw old lads chase him around the yard with pitch forks, and he enjoying it. It was the same that day in Croke Park. He ran at top speed, dancing, prancing, swerving, swaying, dodging, and all the time with that old peaked cap pulled well down over his eyes. He played with a smile on his face and a twinkle in his eye. Magic!

In the Sunday Press that weekend, there was a large photo of Christy Ring, and underneath was written,

"The greatness of Ring will never be forgotten, but Tim Flood is now the greatest forward playing the game, and if the ten Wexford men, who were the mainstay of Leinster's win, had five of their own county colleagues on the team, they would still beat the pick of Munster."

We saw Nickey Rackard, too, in all his glory; so different to Tim Flood, but equally as exciting and as effective. He was so relaxed and confident, but so hungry for the ball and for scores. Mick Dunne wrote in the Sunday Press, *"There was no answer from the mighty south to big Nick's neat points and his powerful crashing goals that had the net behind goalkeeper Tony Reddin almost ripped from its steel mountings"*.

Another writer put it this way, "Flood and Rackard, the 'Terrible Twins' of Wexford hurling, made life miserable for the hard-pressed Munster backs at Croke Park yesterday. Flood, so fast and elusive his direct opponent was left snatching at shadows, and Rackard just demolished the stonewall Munster defence." Every man on the Leinster team played well that day and such a fine win was a boost to hurling in the Province. It convinced the people of Wexford, and especially the players, that they had the winning of the League and the Championship in their own hands now; but you try not to build your hopes and dreams too high.

It was in the days and weeks after the Railway Cup final that I began to appreciate the magnificent spectacle that we had in this game of hurling, and it was almost frightening to think of what could happen in the next six months. I had seen five of my neighbours and boyhood friends perform at a standard I never thought possible in the game I now know to be the greatest field game in the world. My great worry at that time was, would I ever regain a permanent place on this great team? I had played in almost every game since we won the All-Ireland and I was convinced I was good enough, but my dilemma was, there were fifteen fellows better than me. After the defeat in the All-Ireland of '54, I felt I had let people down by not being fit and playing well enough to get my place on the team and be of help. I made a vow that if the opportunity ever came again, I would be ready. By being a sub in '55, I had got my All-Ireland Medal, but it's very different when you are on the team and play your full part in the game.

In preparation for the League Final against Tipperary, we travelled to Portlaoise and played a tournament game against Clare. And Kilkenny came to Enniscorthy and played us a practice two weeks before the final. As the day of the game approached, the press men were finding it hard to say outright that Tipperary would beat Wexford, but, reading between the lines, you could see that was how they were thinking. When asked in an interview with the press before the game, Phil Purcell, who was the manager and trainer of the Tipperary team, said he would believe Wexford could beat Tipperary in a National Final, when he saw it on the scoreboard after the game. In hind sight, I think Mr. Purcell should have kept his thoughts to himself.

If you ask Wexford hurling fans who were lucky enough to be around in the '50s, where they were on 6 May '56, they might not be able to tell you. But if you asked them where they were on the day Wexford beat Tipperary after being fifteen points down at half time, they would tell you right away. This League Final was the most unforgettable game of all the games this great Wexford team played. For the Wexford supporter, the first half was an embarrassing nightmare, but the second-half team-performance by their heroes was the kind of stuff one dreams of. To score 5 goals and 8 points in 30 minutes, against what were probably the best and most experienced backs and goalkeeper ever to play the game, was incredible.

I had better mention the record of this Tipperary team. They had won the League in '54 when they beat Kilkenny, 3.10 to 1.04, and they beat a Wexford team, without the Rackards, in '55, by two goals. They came back again in '57, to win the League. Eight or nine of their team had won three All-Ireland Medals each, so they knew their way around Croke Park.

When the Wexford team to play against Tipperary was selected, there was one change from the team that played against Galway in the All-Ireland Final the previous September. Tom Dixon was on instead of Paddy Kehoe. Many people were surprised, as Paddy was still playing very well, even though he was now thirty four years old.

The team was:

Art Foley

Bobby Rackard	Nick O'Donnell	Mick O'Hanlon
Jim English	Billy Rackard	Mick Morrissey

Jim Morrissey   Seamus Hearne

Padge Kehoe	Ned Wheeler	Tim Flood
Tom Ryan	Nickey Rackard	Tom Dixon

Wexford won the toss and decided to play against the strong wind. More than forty six thousand people had come from all over the country to see the game, and the vast majority were there to see Wexford, and to see them win. The reason for Wexford's dismal display in the first half of this game, I have never heard discussed by the players, but it was humiliating and our supporters must have felt sick. It was suggested by one press man, prior to the game, that Tipperary and all Munster were hurt after the Railway Cup Final by a headline in one paper that said, "Leinster men win with a smile on their faces, and sixteen points to spare". Whatever the reason, Tipperary started the game with all guns blazing, and Wexford didn't know what hit them.

In the first minute the Wexford backs fouled and Paddy Kenny sent over his first point. Paddy scored 2-07 before the game ended, but it still wasn't enough. Tipperary played their own brand of aggressive ground hurling and Wexford had no answer. Seamus Bannon and Liam Devaney scored points, before Paddy Kenny had his first goal, after just nine minutes. Pat Stakelum and Paddy Kenny each scored two points from placed balls. With ten minutes left in the first half, Wexford brought Wheeler to centerfield and Seamus Hearne went centre forward on Pat Stakelum. Jim English got hit on the head and had to come off. Ted Bolger came on to replace him at wing back, but nothing changed.

With the wind in their backs, Tipperary were rampant and could do nothing wrong. Larry Keane, Seamus Bannon and Theo English all scored points, before Tom Ryan got Wexford's only score, a point, in the first half. To make things much worse for Wexford, Paddy Kenny scored his second goal just on the stroke of half time, to leave the score, 2-10 to 0-01. The Wexford supporters were gone almost silent as their team trudged towards the dressing room. One Wexford woman said later that after the match she couldn't find the Tipperary fellow who kept asking at half time, "Will Wexford be brazen enough to come out for the second half?"

When the team came back into the dressing room at half time, it was quiet, with an eerie feeling and men speaking in whispers. It was like as if there had been a bad accident outside and no one knew exactly what to do. The first loud voice was that of Nickey Rackard when he said, "Whoever

wants to use the toilets, go now!" Nickey had four false teeth
in the front of his mouth that time, and he was very conscious
of how bad and wicked he looked without them. So much so,
that he never took them out until just before the ball was
thrown in at the start of the game, and he would have
someone waiting with a handkerchief to take them from him.
This person would run to him with the teeth again as the half
time whistle blew; and so it would be at the start and end of
the second half. He didn't want to have his photo taken
without his teeth.

**Nickey Rackard - always
in command.**

Whatever went wrong on this
day, Nickey had no front teeth in
in the dressing room at half time
and, to add to his unsightly
appearance, there was more
than a trickle of blood on one
side of his face. He was like a
lion in a cage as he paced to and
fro, waiting until every player
was within earshot. Then he
broke the silence in no uncertain
way. I don't remember
everything he said, but some I
remember well. He drew on the
table so hard with his hurl that
every bag and bottle jumped six
inches, and he said, "For Christ's
sake lads, what's gone wrong
with us. Are we paralysed or
what? What's gone on out there
is wrong. We're a bloody
disgrace, and that includes
meself. We can't do this to
ourselves, and we can't do it to

the thousands of Wexford people out there who are with us in
this and who have been with us for the past five years. We
have dug a hole for ourselves, and we must get out of it.
There is no way I'm going back to Wexford tonight if we don't
go out now and make a fight of this. Everything we have
done is lost if we let these fellas beat us by five goals. Anyone
who read the papers last week knows that there are still
people out there who question our worth and our right to be
called Champions. Phil Purcell said he would believe
Wexford could beat Tipperary in a National Final when he
saw it on the scoreboard after the game".

Again, Nickey shook the bottles on the table with his hurl,
and said, "For Christ's sake lads, let us go out there now and
change this forever. If we go out now and fight to the bitter
end and beat these fellows, we'll be the greatest team that
ever came into Croke Park. We have lost sweat and blood to
get to where we are, and we must not give up now. Think of
our fathers and mothers and every Wexford man who died in
'98. This is wrong, lads! We mustn't do this to ourselves.
Tipperary are playing great hurling out there. Are we going
to stand back and look at them for another half hour. By God,
we're not! Who are the bloody All-Ireland Champions, is it
them or us? We are the Champions, so let us get out there
now and prove it!"

There was a mad scramble for the door, so much so, that
players could have injured each other getting out. Nickey
may have been the only player on the way into the dressing
room who still believed we could win this game, but, on the
way out, everyone believed it. I'll never forget the face of the
County Board Chairman, Sean Browne, as he listened to
Nickey speak in the dressing room that day. Sean was a very
sensitive man who worried about small things. He had a face
like Peter Ustinov, and he stood there biting his lower lip and
the tears running down his cheeks. I think what Nickey said

that day convinced the players that they had three options: they could play as they did in the first half and be humiliated; they could up their game and, with the help of the wind, make the scoreboard look respectable and put the defeat down to a bad day at the office; or they could do what they knew in their hearts Nickey wanted them to do, and that was to play as they had never done before and win the game. To win would make them one of the greatest teams of all time. To lose would leave them just another team that happened to win an All-Ireland. They chose to win the game, and the rest is history.

As one of the five subs that day, I was sitting in the dug-out with the selectors, the team doctor, the hackney drivers and an accumulation of other so-called officials and hangers-on. There was no real dug-out, just some of the sideline seats that were reserved for the subs and mentors. As the second half of the game took shape and Wexford clawed their way back into contention, it would have been as easy to get injured in the dug-out as on the field of play. Wexford needed to score fifteen points just to draw level. That would be one point every two minutes. It was a race against the clock.

When the Wexford team emerged from the dressing room after half time, they looked confident and business like, and there was a mighty roar from the fans when they saw Paddy Kehoe was on for the second half. Paddy went out wing-forward, Tim Flood went centre forward and Seamus Hearne was wing-back, in place of Ted Bolger. We now had our best six forwards on and it was obvious we were going to attack at all costs. Tim Flood had one eye almost closed from an injury he got in the first half, and that was a worry as the second half got under way. After two minutes of ferocious attacking, Wexford got their first score. Tim Flood went high for a ball and soloed a bit before he passed to Paddy Kehoe, Paddy crossed to Nickey who burst his way through a couple of

backs and palmed the ball into the net. This brought the
Wexford fans to life and they saw it as a foretaste of what
could happen.

The Tipperary men, too, saw it as a warning and they
upped their defiance. So much so, that the tackles became
brutal, but fair. Paddy Kenny scored a point for Tipperary,
which should have settled them down a bit, but our lads
changed gear again and Tom Ryan scored a goal. Only five
minutes of the second half had gone yet, and Morrissey and
Wheeler had taken over completely at centre field. The
Tipperary puck-out was dropping short and the two lads
were onto it like bees on a pot of honey. Jim Morrissey was
fouled and, instead of waiting for the usual free-taker to come
up, he picked the ball up and hit it over the bar himself.
There was no time to lose now. Wheeler sent over a point
from more than 70 yards. Padge Kehoe sent over a great
point, and Tipperary's lead was cut to seven points, after only
ten minutes.

The Wexford backs were still coming under fierce pressure
as Tipperary tried to stem the tide. Paddy Kenny, who was
rampant throughout this whole game, got a free and sent
over another point, to give his team an eight point lead again.
For a minute we thought, had our lads shot their bolt, but
there was still lots of time. Wheeler and Jim Morrissey
(twice) sent over wonderful points from far out. Now we were
only five points behind and fifteen minutes left. The Wexford
fans were going wild as they got the scent of victory, but this
great Tipperary team found another gear and Paddy Kenny
gave them a six point lead again. For five minutes, they held
Wexford scoreless. For those five minutes the battle raged
and the crowd roared, but there was no score.

What went on in the dug-out for those few minutes, I'll
never forget. In those days, there were women who would
move through the crowd at games, selling oranges and

chocolate from big wicker baskets which they carried on their arms. Well, one such lady came pushing her way through the seats in the dug-out, as the battle raged on the park. She was getting all kinds of abuse as she shouted, "The last few bars of chocolate". As she struggled to get past Doctor Daly the poor man lost his cool and, with his clenched fist, he drew up on the basket and scattered oranges and chocolate all over the place. Without blinking an eye, the woman grabbed the heavy basket by the handle and, three times, she drew down on the Doc's head, as she shouted, "You black ignorant culchie". She then turned her attention to one of the selectors and said "What are you smiling about?" and she hit him one too, before she moved off.

Both teams dug deep for those five scoreless minutes, and the tackles were as hard as I have ever seen. One or two by the Tipperary backs were a bit over the top, and one of the Wexford hackney drivers, who was always inclined to get over-excited, left his seat and was heading in on the field to sort things out himself until the Doc followed him and brought him back to his seat. Slowly but surely, Wexford were getting the better of the exchanges, especially the backs where Bobby Rackard was giving an exhibition reminiscent of his display in the All-Ireland final of '54.

With ten minutes to go, after good work by Padge Kehoe and Nickey Rackard, Tom Dixon got in to flick the ball past Tony Reddan, and there were now only three points between the teams. Wexford's jubilation was cut short again, when Paddy Kenny scored what could be the insurance point for Tipperary. Within a minute, Padge Kehoe, with a great ground shot, brought Tipperary's lead back to three points. As the game entered the last five minutes, everyone started watching the clock. One of the Wexford forwards was fouled. Nickey raced out, took the free, and the lead was down to two points.

The next three minutes was the only time I have ever felt physically sick while watching a sporting event. After such a phenomenal and heroic effort, was time going to run out on us? Two more minutes of sheer hell passed as Wexford bombarded the Tipperary goal, searching for the winning score. I heard someone say there are three minutes left as Tom Ryan raced out under Hill 16 to collect the ball and, as he stooped down, an over-zealous Tipperary defender crashed into him. The referee had no hesitation in awarding a free from the 21yd line, close to the side line. Nickey was out in a flash. What would he do? What could he do? It was a difficult decision. Time was ticking away and the crowd went a bit quiet. I have never heard Nickey say what he tried to do; the ball headed straight for the posts, but dropped short and fell at the edge of the square. Tom Dixon was on it in a flash, and the ball was in the net.

We were a point in front and all hell broke loose. Men, who would have you believe they were hard men, were crying now. The excitable hackney man had lost it completely and was dancing twenty yards in on the park and the Doc trying to get him back to his seat. There was still time for Tipperary to salvage something, but, in reality, there wasn't a hope. In less than a minute, Nickey Rackard had the ball in the Tipperary net again. There was still a little time left, but no one seemed to care. Few sports-minded people experience such an outpouring of joy and emotion as was released now. The last two minutes were played in the most bizarre circumstances, with Wexford fans on the side line moving out on the pitch, and those in the stand on their way down to join in the celebrations.

The final score was: Wexford, 5-09, Tipperary, 2 -14, and, like Nickey Rackard said later, we all hoped Phil Purcell had a good long look at the score board after the game. After a long delay, Jim English, with his head swathed in bandages,

Jim English receives the Cup after the League Final in '56.

made his way to the Hogan Stand to receive the cup. In his speech, Jim said how disappointed he was to have had to leave the field and miss playing in such a wonderful game, but, after looking at the game from a different angle, he saw for himself what a great team of men his comrades were.

The Wexford players were never so sore and bruised as they were after this game, but no one was badly injured and that was good as there was still some unfinished business. Most of the struggle for the past six years was forgotten after this game, with some of the experts in the press asking the question, was this the greatest team in the history of hurling? All the pundits were making us favourites to win the All-Ireland now, and the players were happy with that. Without being arrogant, we knew we could beat any team in the country if we stayed injury-free. The celebrations after that League Final were massive, but short lived, as the championship was approaching.

Some of the stories told after that game were funny. One of the press reporters from Enniscorthy said that when Tom Dixon scored the goal that put Wexford in front, he threw his book of notes into the air and never saw them again. I remember, too, that day, how thousands of Wexford fans were still on the street outside when a battered and weary Wexford team emerged from Croke Park. It must have been an hour after the game ending, but they were waiting there just to show their appreciation for what the team had done. Many of them were unable to give a cheer or shout as their voices had gone completely. So they just stood there and clapped their hands. The full Wexford team was elected "Sport Star of the Week", in the *Irish Independent*, for the week following that game and the players were elevated to new heights in the minds of the general public. Many of the players became folk heroes and are still objects of great curiosity to people from all over Ireland who lived through the '50s.

As we looked forward to the championship now, the Wexford supporters could see nothing but big games, big crowds and big results. There were four weeks to the first round of the Leinster Championship, and four months to the All-Ireland Final. The players, too, were very confident, and very conscious of the opportunity they had to go that extra mile and prove to themselves and the hurling world that they were the best team in the country. There were three teams capable of beating us if we weren't at our very best. Kilkenny, Cork and Tipperary would be waiting in the long grass, looking for the first sign of fragility.

We had twenty players, any one of whom would be a huge loss. The two Kehoes, Paddy and Padge, were still playing for the County football team, and that was a bit of a worry; and, to add to the danger, the football team were doing quite well in the championship. From 6 May to 10 June, the Wexford supporters got a short break and a chance to save a few pounds for the championship games that they were looking forward to. We did very little training, but went to London to play Tipperary in an exhibition game, and played a practice match ten days before the first round of the championship.

On 10 June, we were fresh and ready for the first round, which was against Laois. This game was played in Kilkenny on a really hot day, but the Laois team were not at their best and put up very little resistance to a Wexford team that looked very capable of defending their All-Ireland title. The final score, 3-9 to 2-2, was proof that Wexford were still hungry for success. From the team that had played in the League final against Tipperary, Padge Kehoe had been dropped and Oliver Gough was brought in at wing forward. Each player now had to play to his full potential to hold his place on the team, which was a good thing. Kilkenny beat Dublin in the semi-final and qualified to meet Wexford in the Leinster Final on 8 July.

The team did very little training, but we played a round or two of the County championship in the weeks before the Leinster Final. I think this may have confused the selectors, as they made three changes on the team for the Kilkenny game. Ted Morrissey was brought in at corner-back, instead of Mick O'Hanlon, and the two Kehoes were in again to replace Seamus Hearne and Oliver Gough. The situation now was that any of these players could be match winners on their day, so the general public were not too worried who was on or who was off.

The team to play Kilkenny was:

Art Foley

Bobby Rackard	Nick O'Donnell	Tom Morrissey
Jim English	Billy Rackard	Mick Morrissey

Jim Morrissey   Ned Wheeler

Paddy Kehoe	Tim Flood	Padge Kehoe
Tom Ryan	Nickey Rackard	Tom Dixon

Subs: Mick O' Hanlon, Ted Bolger, Martin Codd, Seamus Hearn, Oliver Gough, Pat Nolan.

When the Kilkenny team was announced, there was one new man making his first appearance in a senior Leinster Final. This man was the great Ollie Walsh. We had seen him play at centre field and in the goal for Kilkenny minor teams and were looking forward to seeing him play at senior level. In victory or defeat, Ollie was always a star. As well as being a great goalkeeper, he was also a great showman and could make every save look spectacular and difficult. The game needs more men like Ollie.

The Kilkenny team was:

Ollie Walsh

Jim Hogan	John Maher	Mark Marnell
Paddy Hoban	Paddy Buggy	Johnny McGovern

Willie Walsh   Mick Brophy

PJ. Garvan	Sean Clohessy	J. Murphy
Dick Rockett	Billy Dwyer	Dick Carroll

A record crowd of 52,000 fans came to Croke Park to see this game. Only once had Kilkenny beaten Wexford in the championship in the past five years and they were getting impatient and frustrated, which made them dangerous, but it was Wexford who started with all guns blazing. In less than two minutes, Nickey Rackard sent a rasper past Ollie Walsh and, a minute later, he scored a point from play. A few minutes later, an unexpected and funny incident took place. From the time the game started, Mark Marnell and Tom Ryan had been trying to decide who had the right to stand on the corner of the square. Now, these two fellows would have known each other very well as Tom had played his early club-hurling in Kilkenny, so they probably had a few things to talk about.

Suddenly, a ball dropped down near the corner flag, under Hill 16, and Tom raced off to collect it. Mark followed close behind, and waited until Tom had the ball in his hand; he then took a drive at him to try to put him out over the line, but Tom made the unusual decision to burst past Mark and head off on a solo run along the end line. Tom's solo runs were few and far between and not very graceful. He would remind you of a child with a ball on a tennis racquet; the hops would be like his solo runs, few and far between. He made it to the corner of the square where John Maher took a charge at him, but again, Tom burst by him and crashed the ball to the roof of the net and, without breaking stride, he gave a hop and a skip, as much as to say, "What about that one, lads!".

Padge Kehoe scored a point from far out the field and we were two goals and two points to no score, after just ten minutes. Dick Rockett scored a goal for Kilkenny and Sean Clohessy got a point and then a goal, before Billy Dwyer got the levelling point. Paddy Kehoe scored a point and Nickey got a goal and a point before half time, leaving the score, Wexford 3-04 Kilkenny 2-02.

The second half was fast and furious, with every man playing his part. Ollie Walsh kept his team in the game with some wonderful saves, and Paddy Buggy was performing well at centre back. Jim English, the Wexford captain, was the best man on the field. After some of the best hurling I ever saw, Kilkenny were just two points behind entering the final minute, putting our backs under fierce pressure. Our hearts were in our mouths as we prayed for the final whistle, but when the referee blew his whistle and pointed for a free in for Kilkenny, my heart stopped altogether. This free was just about twenty-one yards out from the Wexford goal, and dead straight in front. I'll never forget the feeling as we saw the referee telling Willie Walsh that he had to score direct, as time was up. There was almost dead silence as Willie lifted and struck a deadly shot for the Wexford net, but someone got his hurl to the ball and it glanced over the bar for a point. The final score was, Wexford, 4-08   Kilkenny, 3-10.

Wexford were now Leinster Champions for the third year in succession, and would play Galway in the All-Ireland semi-final, on 29 July. Our football team, too, had reached the Leinster Final and were to play, on 22 July, against Kildare. There were three of the hurling team still playing for the footballers, and the danger was that one of them might get injured. Paddy Kehoe, Padge Kehoe and Ted Morrissey were the players involved, and they would have just one week to recover after a hard game of football. Forty-eight thousand fans were in Croke Park for the Football Final, and the thousands who travelled from Wexford would be on the road again the following Sunday to support the hurlers. All this travelling was putting a great strain on people's finances, with the result that some shopkeepers and businesses were worried about the amount of credit customers were asking for. The football team played very well in the first half and were ahead by one point at half time, but Kildare came good in the second half and won by six points. The only consolation we had was that the three hurlers came through the game without injury.

While we were watching our footballers play in Croke Park, Cork and Limerick were playing the Munster Hurling Final in Thurles and the winners there would go straight into the All-Ireland Final, as Antrim had decided not to take part in the senior championship. My brother, Pat, was at the game in Thurles that day, so I had a first hand account of the extraordinary finish to the game. Cork had no answer to this very fast Limerick team who were leading, 2-5 to 1-2, entering the last five or six minutes. Christy Ring had been well held and had been starved of possession for the entire game, until the last five minutes when he broke free and took control of the game. He scored three goals and one point and Cork were into the final. It was frightening to think of what he could do if he got a good supply of the ball, but it was too soon to start worrying about that. We had to get over Galway first.

When the selectors sat down to pick the team to face Galway, they changed their minds again about the left corner back and the centre forward positions. Mick O'Hanlon was in again at corner back and Jim Morrissey was centre forward with Seamus Hearn back again at centre field. The feeling in the county was that we could beat Galway and meet Cork in the final, which was what the whole hurling world was looking forward to, but there is always the fear of something going wrong. We need not have worried, because we beat Galway convincingly. This big Wexford team was now at its peak and was so confident that it must have been an ordeal just to face it on the field. Every man in the panel had the skill and the confidence to hold his own in any company, and add to that the leadership of Nickey Rackard and you had a team that was almost unbeatable. Nickey, who was in his seventeenth year playing senior hurling for his county, scored five goals and three points in this game, against a team that was considered to be pretty good. The final score was, Wexford, 5-13 to Galway 1-08.

It would be eight long weeks before Cork and Wexford would face each other in the Hurling Final of '56. No previous sporting occasion got such coverage from press and radio in this country as did this game. On the Monday after Wexford beating Galway, the argument started. Wexford or Cork? Rackard or Ring? Normally, the hurling final was played on the first Sunday of September, but, owing to an outbreak of polio in Cork, this game was postponed until 23 September. This delay gave every scribe and critic time to have his say, but it made it difficult for the players to keep focused and hold the right level of fitness.

There was an old English chap by the name of Joe Sherwood, who wrote a column in the Evening Press every Monday and he had become a great admirer of the Wexford team. He was always trying to get an argument going about something that was topical. On the evening after Wexford beat Galway, he finished his article by saying he reckoned the only way Cork could beat this great Wexford combination was to have them kidnapped or deported a week before the game. I can tell you, that brought a strong reaction from Cork people and he had a very interesting column for the following eight weeks. Mick Dunne, who wrote for the Sunday Press and was very knowledgeable about hurling, asked the question, "Will we ever again see the like of Rackard or Ring?" He then went on to say, "How fortunate we are to have lived through their years of greatness, to have witnessed their fabulous feats and to have seen the splendour of the game as they played it".

There are times when I am asked by today's hurlers, how Rackard and Ring would fit into today's game and under

Our respect for authority and our ability to march properly and stand to attention for our National Anthem was always admired.

Pre-match Parade All-Ireland Final 1956.

today's rules. Well, I honestly think they would do even better today because the changes in the rules favour the skilful forward. There is one thing of which I am certain: no other player of any sport has brought so many people from the four corners of Ireland to watch them play, as Christy Ring and Nickey Rackard did. From all the analysis and all the rubbish that was written in the weeks before this game, one fact emerged, Wexford were favourites and the whole country, with the exception of Cork, wanted Wexford to win. This may have been because Cork had won twenty-two All-Ireland Finals, while Wexford had won only two, but I think there was more to it than that.

This team had a glamour that enticed people to support them. Their average height was just under six feet, and they were very athletic. They were handsome and always well dressed, which helped in its own way. They were renowned for their sportsmanship and fair play, but always gave the impression that if there was what you might call a disturbance, they were well able to look after themselves.

Jim English, Billy Rackard and Jim Morrissey stand to attention for the playing of the National Anthem.

Only twice in eight years did I see one of them sent off by a referee. Their respect for authority and their ability to march properly and stand to attention for our National Anthem when they went to Croke Park, was always admired. All this made them very popular all over the country; but their greatest gift to their people, which almost went unnoticed, was how they helped lift the depression of the poverty and hardship of the '30s and '40s from the people of County Wexford.

The eight weeks before the final proved to be long and anxious for the players and management of the team. The fear was that we could over train, or we might not do enough. It was decided that we would carry on as normal, doing two nights a week and lots of hurling over the weekends. From the pattern of the training sessions, I got an inkling that the selectors were thinking of playing me at centre forward in the final. I must admit that this excited me greatly and changed my whole attitude to training for the next six weeks.

I planned every detail of my life until the day of the game. I would do my normal day's work, but I would go to bed at 10.15pm and get up at 7.30am if at all possible. I would eat well, four times each day. Because I believe in God and the power of prayer, I'd say one small special prayer every day until the day of the match. I'd leave no stone unturned and then, if things didn't go my way, so be it. It was a chance in a million, and I was going to take it. I wasn't to know for certain that I would be playing until two weeks before the game, but Nickey Rackard had asked me how I felt about playing centre forward.

I asked John Randall to make the best hurl he possibly could for me, just in case I was needed. He asked me to call down to him in Killurin whatever night I could and together we would plan the type of stick I needed. Some people were sceptical about John's ability to make special hurls to suit each player's different style, but I had spent many nights discussing the whole art of the game of hurling with John and I had great faith in his work.

If I was selected to play centre forward against Cork, I

would be playing on Willie John Daly, who was a smallish man. I would have six inches of an advantage in height and two stone in weight, so that was a good start. My strongest attribute was my ability to hit the ball high in the air, and that was going to be my main tactic as I knew I was going to be the target man for the puck-out.

Until then, I had been using a thirty-six inch hurl, but John suggested I should use a thirty-seven inch because of my height. The next thing we decided on was the weight of the hurl. John gave me six or eight good hurls, to select the one which I liked best, weight-wise. The boss of the new hurl would be half an inch longer than normal, and the back would be a little wider than the norm. The grip, too, would be changed to facilitate the movement of my huge hands. When the measurements had all been finally decided, John said he didn't have a suitable piece of ash planked, as it was all too heavy to make such a hurl. He needed well-seasoned young ash, and asked me to come back to him again in one week, when he would have some work done on it.

When I went back and saw the hurl, I was surprised, it was a bit heavy and the grip was unfinished, but John explained he still had a lot of work to do. He had finished the grip on another hurl in the style he intended using on mine, and it felt good. The grain in the stick was wide, with just the right amount of spring. There was life in the ash, and I was pleased. John said to come back in two or three days, and he'd have it finished. When I saw the finished product, I couldn't leave it out of my hand. It was a work of art, and it is still one of my most treasured possessions after all these years. About three weeks before the final, we played Kilkenny in a practice match in Wexford Park and I was on at centre forward. I could do nothing wrong, and scored 2-04.

Nickey told me to have myself right for the final, and that they were leaving it to me to do whatever training I thought necessary. This gave me great confidence and lifted the great weight of doubt off my shoulders. It was now up to myself, and I renewed my resolve to do things my own way. I never read a paper, or listened to sports programmes on the radio for the three weeks before the match, as I knew there would be a bit of controversy over my selection. I know some local pundits said the selectors were taking a chance playing me, and I still have a copy of one of the Sunday papers in which Mick Mackey said that the only position where he was sure Cork would have an advantage, was at centre back; but he did say Wexford would win.

I did some hurling every day with my new hurl and trained with the rest of the team until the Monday night before the game. After training we talked about what might go right and what might go wrong. I was told that my principal job was to get the ball inside our half forward line, and turn their half backs. I was so pleased with my new hurl and how I was striking the ball; I said to myself, that's it, I'm right now, so let's wait until Sunday. I always believed in being fresh and eager for a game. It may have been all in the head, but I liked to put away the hurl for four or five days before a big game.

One of the reasons I decided to write this book and tell the story, as best I can, of this Wexford team, is that, with the passing of the years, the story has become folklore. Two years ago I was talking to a man who told me he was a ten year old boy in '56 when we beat Cork. He asked me questions about how I felt going out on Croke Park before a crowd of eighty thousand people, and if I was worried and nervous before the game. Then he told me where he was and who was with him, while the game was going on. He was from a village in the middle of County Wexford and he told me how they had prepared for the game. All except those under twelve and over seventy had gone to Croke Park.

His grandfather, who was in his seventies, but still the jack-of-all- trades in the village, was left in charge. He was the kind of man who would be on the door for every function in the parish hall and on the stage to oversee the night's raffle, and collect the pence in church on Sunday. The village consisted of the church and priest's house, which were on a height over the road, the parish hall, the post office, a small shop and a few houses. The Parish Priest had made his radio, which was a good one, available for the game. This radio was placed on the high wall surrounding the church, with one person delegated to operate it. There were some chairs placed around, and every parishioner was welcome to listen to the game.

Some women were asked to look after the small children, and two men were told to keep the bigger ones quiet. Before the game started, three of the older women said they would go up to the church and say a Rosary, so that no player would be injured and Wexford would win. With Wexford leading well and everything going fine entering the last fifteen minutes, Cork scored a goal and the grandfather got a bit worried, so he asked the three women to go back into the church again and pray. Seven minutes later, Cork had gone in front, and the grandfather went crazy on the road when he saw the three women coming out of the church, so he started shouting and waving his arms at them, "Get back in again quick, we're in trouble". When the game was over and Wexford had won, the grandfather decided he would make a bit of a speech, so he stood up on the steps leading up to the church and he said, "I want to thank the Parish Priest for the use of his radio, and the people who put out the chairs, and a special thanks to Mrs. Murphy, Mrs. Kelly and Mrs. O'Brien; without their prayers I think Cork would have won that match".

The Wexford team that played the All-Ireland Final, in '56, was:

Art Foley

Bobby Rackard   Nick O'Donnell   Mick Morrissey

Jim English   Billy Rackard   Jim Morrissey

Seamus Hearne   Ned Wheeler

Padge Kehoe   Martin Codd   Tim Flood

Tom Ryan   Nickey Rackard   Tom Dixon

Subs: Mick O'Hanlon, Paddy Kehoe, Pat Nolan, Ted Morrissey, Oliver Gough, Ted Bolger.

The Cork team was:

Mick Cashman

Jimmie Brohan   John Lyons   Tony O'Shaughnessy

Matt Fouhy   Willie John Daly   Paddy Philpott

Eamonn Goulding   Paddy Dowling

Mick Regan   Josie Hartnett   Paddy Barry

Christy O'Shea   Terry Kelly   Christy Ring

Wexford brought on no sub, made no positional switch, and no Wexford man went down injured during the game. That must be a record.

Because the '56 Final was for me the best and most memorable game I was ever involved in, it is still fresh in my mind. People of my age will understand when I say it's very difficult to remember things that happened fifty years ago, but what I was doing and how I was thinking in the weeks and days leading up to that game, I remember well. It was not a busy time on the farm, so I was doing some repairs to the cow house. Helping me was a neighbour by the name of Tom Dempsey. Tom was a qualified and skilled tradesman, but had lost his right arm in a road accident when he was in his early twenties. He had learned to work with his left hand and could do as much work in a day as any man. He was a simple gentle soul, with a lovely sense of humour, and to watch him work was inspirational. One day, while Tom and myself were at work, a big black car drove into the yard and out stepped Padraig Puirseil from the *Irish Press*, looking for a photo and a few comments about the game. A few days later, what Tom and myself had to say and a fine photo of both of us at work, appeared in the national press. A copy of that paper was one of Tom's most treasured possessions.

We did no work on Saturday, but got everything ready for the people who would stay at home. Kitty and I had four children under seven years, so someone was going to be busy for the next two days. We had to make sure the radio was working well, and that there was plenty of water up from the well, which was three hundred yards away from the house. Firewood was left ready as much of the cooking was still being done on the open fire. Kitty's mother would be in to help my mother and father with the children, and Tom Dempsey and his wife Nellie would come in to listen to the match and help, if help was needed.

The last thing I did before I went to bed on Saturday night, was pack my bag and make sure I had everything I needed. The last thing I dropped into the bag was a new pair of bootlaces, and I thought of the first time I went to play in Croke Park, when I had no bag at all. The bag I had now was made of leather and had a fine zip fastener and, now that I think of it, I had a spare pair of underpants - on my first visit to Croke Park I had none at all. For weeks, I had been thinking about this game and I had an answer to every eventuality, but still, thoughts kept coming into my head about this and that and the other thing, and this Saturday night was no different.

I had never seen Willie John Daly play in the back line, and I was trying to figure out how he might do things. Many times I had seen him play in the half forward line; he was fast and skilful, but speed is not an advantage when the ball is dropping from the sky. I felt I could win most of the balls that would come between us, and that would be OK. I had Padge Kehoe on my right, Tim Flood on my left, and in front of me, Nickey Rackard. I knew these fellows' play like the back of my hand, so I couldn't go wrong. Those were the thoughts in my head as I fell asleep on Saturday night.

The travel arrangements for Sunday were no different to other trips to games in Croke Park. Martin O'Dwyer picked us up at half nine in the morning and we arrived at the hotel about half past twelve. It was obvious when we reached the city that there would be a record crowd at the game. The streets around Croke Park were crammed with people and the atmosphere was different to what it had been the year before, when we played Galway. The Wexford supporters were really worked up for this one, and it was a relief to reach the quietness of the dressing room. Over 83,000 people paid for admission, but it was estimated that over ten thousand went in for free when one of the gates was forced open.

Micheál O'Hehir's commentary was, for the first time, broadcast live to America and Africa. I think the reason it was broadcast to Africa was because there were so many Irish Missionaries there at that time.

The first time I felt a bit of pressure was while we were going from the car to the dressing room. The nightmare of '54 when Wexford had played the better hurling, but Cork won the game in the last few minutes, was still fresh in my mind. My brother, Pat, was at the Munster Final and he told me how Ring had scored those three goals in the last five minutes when it looked as if Limerick had the game won. Could Ring, or someone else, do that kind of thing again today? Those were the thoughts that began to enter my head, but when I thought of the League Final against Tipperary, the confidence was back again.

The dressing room was calm, with that eerie feeling of anticipation and no one saying much. I remember when we sat down to tog off for the game, Tim Flood said to me, "This is the big one. If we can win this one we are made for ever."

And how right he was! This was the supreme test. Eleven of this Cork team had won three finals in a row, '52, '53 and '54. Wexford had twelve of the team who were beaten by Cork in '54.

The last fifteen minutes before we left the dressing room seemed so very long. I picked up my socks and my tie just to keep my hands steady, and put them in my bag, and then I saw my new pair of bootlaces and thought to myself, I should have put them in my boots in case the old ones would break. I never tied my laces until we were ready to leave the dressing room, so I had time to change them. George Ryan, who usually travelled with the Enniscorthy lads, was in the dressing room and he came to help me. I had never seen such a long pair of laces and George had a unique way of lacing and tying the boots. My boots never felt so comfortable, and it all helped.

I had played before some huge crowds, but nothing could prepare you for the shock of going out on Croke Park before a crowd of 90,000 frenzied fans on All-Ireland Hurling Final day. There was very little said in the dressing room before the game, but everyone knew the task that we faced. We had more to beat than fifteen Cork men. We had to beat the unknown. We had twenty one players who were prepared to rise above any eventuality. The victory over Tipperary in the League final had dispelled any shadow of doubt or inferiority complex that remained in the minds of the players and supporters. This would be the crowning victory for the team that gave more joy and pleasure to Wexford people than any other team who set foot in Croke Park before.

We never raced from the dressing room onto the park, as most teams do now. It may have been that we wanted to save our energy for the game, but we just ran out in a business-like fashion and pucked a few balls about to get the feel of the park and the surroundings. I have been sometimes asked by young players what it is like to emerge from the tunnel on to the park on these occasions. There is no easy answer to that question, because I'm sure it affects different players in different ways.

By 1956, we had been coming to Croke Park five or six times each year for seven years, so most of the players would have played up to forty games there. This would have made it like our home ground. What made it different for the '56 final was the size of the crowd and the importance of the game. During the parade I remember looking at the crowd as we marched around the park. At both ends and under the Cusack Stand, where it was standing room only, there was a sea of faces. There were people on the roof of the stands, and perched on every available wall and pole. There was a continuous roar as we passed by each section of the grounds. The only time there was silence was for the playing of the National Anthem and it was during this time I discovered the real meaning of the phrase, "Knocking at the knees".

Always the one to take up the front position for the throw in, Christy Ring got in the first stroke and sent the ball up to Billy Rackard. Billy was fouled as he was clearing his line and took the free himself. He hit a long high ball up to me,

The throw-in at the start of the final in 1956.
A sea of faces in the background.

on the forty yard line, and I doubled on it in the air, to my left. Tim Flood was on it in a flash, and we were one point up in less than half a minute. Any nervousness that the big occasion had created in my mind, disappeared in that one half minute, and now it was just another serious game of hurling. For two minutes the ball flew up and down the field, with both sets of backs just about holding out. There were no wides and just one line-ball to each team. Padge Kehoe collected a poor clearance from the Cork backs and, from twenty five yards, sent the ball to the roof of the Cork net, with only three minutes gone. The game was on five minutes when Cork got their first score, a pointed free from Ring. Scores were hard to come by at this stage of the game, with both sets of backs playing well.

With eleven minutes gone, Tim Flood set off on a solo run up his own wing and when he was tackled, he passed the ball to me as I ran up the centre. The pass was a bit short and I had to check my run, but I tapped it over the bar as it hopped. If the pass had come in front of me I felt I would have scored a goal as I was just fourteen yards out. Cork's captain, Tony O'Shaughnessy, retired injured at this stage and was replaced by veteran defender, Vin Twomey. The game was on for sixteen minutes when Cork got their first score from play, which was a point by Mick Regan. In the next five minutes we scored four points from play. Nickey Rackard, Tim Flood (twice) and Tom Dixon all scored. In the last eight minutes of the first half we got no score, while Cork got two pointed frees from Ring and one from play by Eamonn Goulding, which was a bit worrying. With the half time score, 1-6 to 0-5, in our favour, we should have been happy enough, but we were disappointed we hadn't scored more.

We felt we were having the best of the exchanges all over the field, but the scoreboard is what counts at the end. The feeling in the dressing room at half time was, if we didn't get more scores quickly we could be in trouble at the end. Ring had got no score from play in the first half, but while he was on the pitch no lead was safe. He had destroyed Limerick in the last five minutes of the Munster Final, and we knew he was capable of doing the same to us. The only plan we had for the second half was to play as we did in the first half, and increase our lead as much as possible. We knew Cork would make one supreme effort at some stage during the second half, and the advice was not to panic. Nickey Rackard's last words were, "We know we can beat these fellas, but we still have to do it. The danger is, they will come at us late, and we won't have time to react. We are the best team, so, when they lift their game let us do the same".

The second half started again at a ferocious pace, but there was no score for five minutes. We were still having the best of the exchanges, but we had three wides before Nickey got a point from a free. Within two minutes of that, we got two more points. Billy Rackard scored one from a seventy, and I got one from play. With eight minutes of the second half gone, we were seven points in front and looked to be in command. Then a string of events took place that turned the game on its head and set Croke Park on fire. We were into the fourteenth minute when one of the Cork players sent in a high lobbing ball right into the square. Art Foley moved out and jumped high and caught the ball in his left hand, while Christy Ring came in from the left and jumped a fraction later than Artie. In his effort to catch the ball, Ring caught Art's hurl in his left hand and, as both players landed on the ground, it was plain to see that Art had the ball and Christy still had a grip on Art's hurl.

The ref raced in and everyone in Croke Park thought it was a free out to Wexford, but the ref pointed for a 21 yard free to Cork. He may have penalised Nick O'Donnell for holding Josie Hartnett, but, whatever the free was for, it

Art Foley, Billy Rackard, Jim Morrissey, Mick Morrissey, Nick O'Donnell and Bobby Rackard were not properly lined up for Ring's quickly taken free in the 1956 All-Ireland Final.

changed the course of the game. For a split second, our backs lost their concentration and, before they had lined the goal, Ring had the ball in the net and our lead was cut to four points. There was an almighty roar from the Cork fans, while the Wexford supporters were still letting the ref know they didn't agree with his decision.

Within half a minute Ring scored a point from play and there was only a goal in it. From the puck out, Padge Kehoe went on a solo run and sent over a point from far out to steady the ship. The crowd were going wild now as Cork attacked again and Paddy Barry got a point. Cork were gaining control of the game, and, for the first time, their supporters were winning in the stands and on the terraces. Three more minutes went by without a score, and then Paddy Barry got through for Cork's second goal and the teams were level. One more minute and Cork were in front when Ring raced by Bobby Rackard and, even though under severe pressure, he palmed the ball over the bar.

While the Cork fans were going wild I remember taking a look at the scoreboard at the railway end, and noticed Nickey

Rackard coming away out from his full forward position, roaring at us to get the ball down there. I couldn't really hear what he was saying, but I knew from past experience what his message would be. From the puck out, Cork went on the attack again as Terry Kelly sent in a high ball which Art Foley caught and cleared to centre field. Seamus Hearne got possession and crossed to where Padge Kehoe and Paddy Philpott clashed. The ball broke to me and I flicked it to where I knew Nickey was waiting, unmarked. He had time to gather the ball and steady himself, and the teams were level again. Cork had been in the lead for less than one minute and Wexford moved up a gear again. Seamus Hearne. who was our Man of the Match, and Tim Flood seemed to move up two gears as they began to race at the Cork defence.

For three minutes, there were wides at both ends as both teams strove for supremacy. Tim Flood got possession near midfield and went on a run near the side line. His marker, whom he had left for dead, threw his hurl at him and gave away the free. It was fifty yards out from goal and near the side line. Nickey came out to take it and, with the greatest of ease, sent the ball over the bar and we were back in front again. For three minutes, now, the ball flew up and down the field, but never crossed the side line. Nickey Rackard had one shot at the posts, but it was inches wide. Christy Ring, under fierce pressure from Bobby Rackard, got in one shot, but it, too, was wide. For those three minutes, there was a continuous roar from 90,000 demented people as each player strained every muscle and sinew in his body, to gain the upper hand.

Eventually, Tom Dixon was taken down by one of the Cork defenders as he was bearing down on the Cork goal, and we had another free, right in front of the posts. Nickey tapped over the point and we were two in front, with three minutes left. We were now in the situation we feared we might find ourselves: two points up, with time running out, and Ring, like a hungry panther, moving out from his position and he roaring for the ball. Mick Cashman hit a mighty puck-out straight down the field, but Billy Rackard sent it back again. Ring moved out the field further, and was around the forty yards mark when a long clearance from the Cork backs came down between Billy Rackard and Terry Kelly. They both pulled hard and the ball broke to Ring.

With every Cork man and woman in the stand on their feet, he raced through the Wexford defence until he reached the 21 yd line and, with no one to beat only the goalie, he let fly a shot for what he, and thousands more, thought would be the winning score; but somehow, Art Foley got his hurl to the ball and it spun into the air. With two of the forwards descending on him, Art batted the ball out to Mick Morrissey, before he was unceremoniously bundled into the back of the goal. Before he got to his feet, Ring was in, grabbed him by the hair of the head and said, "You little black bastard, you've

**One of Art Foley's fine clearances in the All-Ireland '56 Final.
Mick Morrissey is coming in by the goalpost.**

beaten us", and, with that, they shook hands as Art got to his feet and Christy went looking for another chance.

In a matter of seconds, Mick Morrissey's clearance was sent back in again to Art. This time it was a high lobbing ball and, with no one near him, Art had time to catch it and have a good look down the field. Jim English was running loose, fifty yards out, and near the side line. He collected Art's clearance, and he, too, had time to have a look. He hit a long ball in over the heads of the backs and forwards; Tom Ryan was the first to reach it and he saved it from going wide. Knowing that time was almost up, Tom was in no hurry to play the ball. He picked it up and pretended he was going to burst past Vin Twomey, but instead, he dropped the ball and went back and stood over it again for a second. He picked it up again, and, by now, Nickey Rackard had left John Lyons on the edge of the square and raced out to the fourteen yards line, shouting at Tom to pass the ball to him. Tom obliged, with a long high hand-pass over Vin Twomey's head, and Nickey jumped and caught it.

I can remember what happened next the same as if it happened yesterday. As Nickey came down with the ball, one of the Cork outfield players was charging at him. Nickey checked and let him go by. By now John Lyons had seen the danger and was coming out to tackle Nickey. I was coming in at speed and, as you could use the third man tackle at that time, I took John out as he was getting very close to Nickey. I hit him as hard as I ever hit anyone, and both of us fell, right in front of Nickey as he began his swing. I dropped flat on the ground, in fear of blocking his shot, and turned my head towards the goal to see where the ball went. I saw it hit the net about three feet inside the far goalpost. The blast of sound from the Wexford supporters almost burst my ear drums as I jumped to my feet. For a few seconds it looked as if the pitch would be invaded, but, to be honest, I can't remember much more.

Jim English receiving the Cup from the President of the GAA Mr. Seamus McFerran after the '56 Final. The girl at his left shoulder was his then girlfriend and now his wife Maggie.

In the remaining minute, Tom Dixon scored a point, so we won by six points. When the final whistle blew, it seemed the crowd just closed in on us, and, for me, it became very emotional. I know Nick O'Donnell and Bobby Rackard carried Christy Ring on their shoulders from the field, but I didn't see that. I don't remember the presentation of the cup, or how long it was before I got to the dressing room. I do remember the difficulty I had in holding on to my hurl. People asked me to give it to them for a souvenir, while others tried to pull it from my hand. I was so much afraid I would

1956 All-Ireland Hurling Champions

These are the men who played in the All-Ireland Final of 1956. There were no subs introduced, no positional switches made and no players went down injured for the hour. That must be a record.

Back row: Billy Rackard, Nick O'Donnell, Ned Wheeler, Jim Morrissey, Martin Codd, Nickey Rackard, Padge Kehoe, Bobby Rackard, front row: Tom Ryan, Mick Morrissey, Jim English, Art Foley, Tim Flood, Tom Dixon, Seamus Hearn.

lose it, I gave it to a man I scarcely knew, and asked him to give it to someone in the dressing room. There was a split, six inches long, on the front of the boss of the hurl and, when I got it back, this bit was missing, but I am glad I still have the remainder of it. The feeling in the dressing room after the game was of pride and defiance, and our supporters felt the same. When we beat Galway the year before, the feeling was of relief.

Again, we had all the celebrations and all the speeches, but this year it was very different. There was no doubt in anyone's mind that we would go down in history as a great team of entertainers. We had beaten Kilkenny, Tipperary and Cork in the major competitions, which proved we were great hurlers too. The journey home to Wexford on Monday evening was, again, very emotional, but very joyful too. I don't think there are words to describe how one feels at a time like this.

Recently I was at a wedding, and got talking to a man I hadn't met before. He was about my own age and was a very genuine hurling man. We talked about the old days and I said to him, "Did you hurl, yourself?" Now this man was from the north of the county, where there was very little hurling in the '50s. He looked me straight in the face and said, "I played full back for the club in fourteen junior championships and, not alone did we never win a medal, but we never won a match." When you hear stories like that, you're thankful you were born in the right place at the right time. Hurling has been good to me and my family and, no matter how much I put back into the game, it would be only a fraction of what I got out. If I could put a value on the outcome of my involvement in hurling, especially with the team of the '50s, it would be immense. Money can not buy good memories, and memories cannot be erased from one's mind. Sixty years of involvement in the game has left me with great memories,

Jim English arrives back in Enniscorthy with the Cup.

great friends and hope for the future.

In the days and the weeks after we beat Cork, it was back to the celebrations as it was in '55. Every parish organised some kind of function and invited two or three of the players so that the children and the old folks could get a closer look at their heroes. These functions were usually very enjoyable and often very funny. It was an opportunity for the politicians, the Parish Priest and those in high places to express their views on a subject in which they were not always very well versed.

One of the lads tells the story of how he was invited to one of these functions in the south of the county and was to have been seated beside one of the special guests who was a big business man in the locality. For some reason, this man was unable to attend so his wife was deputising for him. This lady was English-born and educated, and had very little knowledge of what the function was all about, but they were introduced to each other and sat down for the meal. My friend would tell the story like this, "This big stout woman was sitting beside me and I couldn't make out a word she was saying. She had a very posh accent and spoke as it she had a very hot potato in her mouth. After a few attempts to get a conversation going, she said to me, "Have you been to England?" "Oh, yes," I said, "we've made several trips to London." "Oh, how nice!" she said, "I presume you have played at Lord's then." "Oh, many times", I said, "many times, Mam."

My most amusing experience was when I visited the school in Rathnure and a young lad said to me, "My daddy said you shouldn't be on the team at all to play Cork because you're too soft and you had no cut in you, and Willie John Daly would cut lumps out of you." I said to him, "When you go home, ask your daddy did he find any of the lumps that Willie John cut out of me." I am still waiting for the answer.

**Panel of '56 with County Secretary and Chairman and
all Trophys that they won.**
Back row: Paddy Kehoe, Martin Codd, Bobby Rackard, Tom Ryan,
Nick O'Donnell, Ned Wheeler, Jim Morrissey, Nickey Rackard.
Middle row: Sean Browne (County Chairman), Billy Rackard, Padge
Kehoe, Mick Morrissey, Jim English, Art Foley, Seamus Hearne, Liam
Murphy (secretary). Front row: Tom Dixon, Mick O'Hanlon, Pat
Nolan and Ted Bolger. Tim Flood is missing from the photo.

Every time Nickey Rackard spoke in the dressing room or
at functions around the country, he would always refer to our
wonderful supporters and say how much it meant to the
players to know that the support was always there, even
when things went wrong. Many of our supporters made huge
sacrifices to get to games all over the country. With the
majority of our games played in Croke Park, the train was
the ideal way to travel, but some people had to cycle ten or
fifteen miles to a railway station, and this would mean early
mornings and late nights.

Two weeks after the All-Ireland Final, we played Limerick
in the semi-final of the Oireachtas Cup. The game was
played in Wexford Park and we won, 8-07 to 1-05. One week
later, we played Kilkenny in the final of the Walsh Cup. This

game was played in Bellefield, in Enniscorthy, and again we won, 2-10 to 1-08. Huge crowds were attending all these games, but, sooner or later, it would all have to come to an end. It was costing our supporters a lot of time and money and, even though the players had no serious injuries, the appetite for the game was beginning to wane.

Seven days after the Walsh Cup Final, we had to face Kilkenny again in the Oireachtas Cup Final. We had won every other competition in '56, so we would make one final effort to make a clean sweep. On 21 October, close to forty thousand people went to Croke Park and saw this panel of players win for the last time on the sacred turf of Jones's Road, where they had entertained over half a million people with their skill and courage. Wexford won the Oireachtas Cup for the fourth time, with the score, 0-16 to 1-09, and, only for the brilliance of Ollie Walsh in the Kilkenny goal, we might have scored five goals. We had now won the five major competitions in '56, and ten of our team had won Railway Cup Medals with Leinster. We had set attendance records for finals in every competition, and we got credit for being one of the most sporting teams ever to play in Croke Park, which is something we were very proud of.

In the dressing room after the Oireachtas Cup Final, Sean Browne, the County Chairman, asked for a bit of silence and then asked the question, would the team be prepared to fly to New York the following May, to play a couple of exhibition games? For a moment there was a stunned silence and then someone blurted out, "Oh Jasus, Sean, we'd go tomorrow morning!" and that was the feeling of every player. A plane trip to America at that time was like going to heaven and, for me personally, it was a dream come true. My mother was born and reared in America, but her memories of the land of her birth were not good.

The League campaign of '56-'57 was not taken too

seriously. We played a draw with Waterford, Kilkenny beat us by two points and Cork beat us by three, in Cork. Some young lads were brought into the team and were doing very well. Oliver (Hopper) McGrath, Jimmie O'Brien and John Nolan all started their careers that winter, and went on to win All-Irelands later.

The US trip was in the balance for a few months, with some saying it could be called off. First, it had to get the all-clear from Central Council and then there was the question of who was going to finance it. On the first Sunday of January we played Kilkenny in Ferns, to raise money to build a new church in Kilrush and, after the game, we were told the trip had got the go-ahead at a meeting of Central Council the night before. Nickey Rackard was Wexford's representative on Central Council, and it was only after he had made an emotional plea that the proposition was passed, with a two thirds majority.

Mid-March came and there was still a shortage of cash to finance our trip and, as far as I can remember, it was the Wexford Men's Association in New York who guaranteed the money. I had my own scare that March, when I had to go into hospital to have my appendix removed. I was in hospital for two weeks and was told by the doctor not to lift anything or ride a bicycle for three months. He never mentioned hurling, so I told everyone I could play again in two months time.

As we prepared for the trip, we had a few problems that players would not have today. We had to be vaccinated against smallpox and this made us very sick for a few days. I have never been so sick in my life, as I was for those three or four days. I couldn't bear the light on my eyes so I just went to bed and covered my head under the bedclothes and never ate a bit for three days, which left me very weak. Unlike nowadays, there was no one to sponsor blazers or suits for the players, so we just had to get something light to wear as we were told it could be very warm in New York at that time of year. We also had to find a few pounds for pocket money, but we were promised a few dollars after we played the first game.

New York

Looking back now, I find it difficult to explain why we were so excited about this trip to America. In my innocence at the time, I looked on America and the American people as the great saviours of the free world and the country that gave refuge to our down-trodden and starving fore-fathers. I was judging what living in America was like by what we were seeing on the screens in cinemas around the country and the glamour and glitter that was coming from Hollywood. We were led to believe that everything in America was bigger than anywhere else in the world. We had seen photos of the cars, the buildings, the skyscrapers and the motorways. Up until now, all this was thousands of miles away and, for some of us, in a land we thought we would never see.

As our trip drew closer, we had enquiries from neighbours and people all over Wexford, asking for the name of the hotel in New York, where we would be staying. These people had relatives in different parts of the USA, who would be coming to New York to see us play. Many of these folk would have been in America for many years and, for them, it was going to be a huge occasion. One of my neighbours told me that his brother, who was in the USA for thirty seven years, was taking his family to New York from the west coast for the two weeks we would be there. This kind of news coming from the USA, reminded us of how important this trip was going to be for our fellow-county men and women, American residents, who would be travelling to New York to see us.

At this time too, I discovered I had relatives that I had never even heard of, in New York. This family were born and reared in England, but had emigrated to the USA in the nineteen thirties and some of them had become very wealthy. It was by strange coincidence, I discovered this family existed. While travelling to Australia in late 1956, my brother, Fr Pat, met one member of this family on the liner in which they were travelling. This man was returning to New Zealand, where he lived. A few weeks into the long journey, a list of their fellow travellers was given to the passengers. The name Codd on the list attracted the man's attention and, one morning after Pat had said Mass, he came up and told him he had been born in England and his mother's name was Codd. They exchanged some family information and discovered they were cousins. He mentioned that some of his family had migrated to New York and Pat told him that I was going to New York to play some games of hurling there in May. He contacted his sister in New York and she wrote to me, asking for the name of the hotel where we would be staying so she could contact me when we arrived. Long before we left for America, we began to realise that the trip would not be all fun. From the feedback we were getting from the USA, we knew there would be a huge amount of Wexford exiles and second generation Irish people at these games, so we had to keep ourselves fit, and not let them down.

Because my mother was born in Albany, the capital city of New York State and some miles north of New York City, I foolishly thought I would know a little about the place and the lifestyle there. My mother's parents had died when she was very young and she had spent a few years in a orphanage before being brought to Ireland, when she was thirteen years old, to be reared by an aunt. She had been taught to play the piano and sing all the old American songs. She would proudly play and sing the American National Anthem, which gave me the feeling I was part-American. As our trip drew closer, I almost felt I was going home. The people checking our papers and passport at the airport seemed pleased when they saw my mother was an American citizen. I still remember, somewhere on our journey, a lady was taking our finger prints and, when she took my thumb in her hand and dipped it in the ink, she was amazed at the size of the print it left on the paper, so much so, that she called her colleague to have a look at the size of my thumb. I almost said something naughty, but I thought I better not.

The team and officials assembled in New Ross on Wednesday, 29 May, to go on an adventure, a mission and an expedition all rolled into one. The players were now fully aware of the great responsibility that was being placed on their shoulders again. When first the trip was sanctioned, we thought of a great two week holiday, but that had changed a bit now. There would be at least thirty thousand people coming to see us play, we were told. The team was proud of their achievements both on and off the field, and were always well groomed in public; and this day in New Ross, they certainly turned a few heads and brought smiles to the faces of their adoring fans, especially the ladies. We had been warned that the weather would be very hot in New York and we would need to wear light-weight clothes, and light in colour too, so many of us looked more like returned Yanks than fellows who were going to the States for the first time. It was all a bit of a laugh for the hundreds of people who were there to cheer as we made our way across the bridge, on the first leg of our journey.

When we arrived at Shannon Airport there were lots of people there to wish ourselves, and the Cork team, good luck on our journey. Both teams were travelling on the same plane, which was good. The Tyrone football team, who were Ulster Champions at that time, flew out to New York just before us. They were going to play a New York selection on the same day as we would play Cork in the Polo Grounds. All three teams would stay in the same hotel. We flew out from Shannon at 3am. on Thursday, 30 May, and it took us nine hours to reach Gander, in Newfoundland. We were flying into a strong wind, we were told, and that was slowing us down,

so one of the wise guys said we'd have to stop for another sup
of petrol. We were allowed to get off the plane for one hour
and, in our light clothes, we felt very cold. When we got back
up in the air, the wind seemed to have got worse and the
plane began to rock a bit. So much so, that some of the lads
began to get a bit nervous, but Paddy Kehoe assured them
that everything was OK, it was only that the pilot didn't
know his job very well and he forgot to push in the choke! It
took us five more long hours to reach New York, so everyone
was very tired.

Because my visa was different, I was the first to get
through the customs and the first to get outside the terminal
building. As I stepped out into the public waiting-area, two
men from the welcoming party rushed to shake my hand, and
a lone trumpeter in the waiting crowd, began to play the
great Wexford air, "Boolavogue". For one full minute, which
is the time it takes to play one verse of "Boolavogue", the
crowd standing about went very quiet and I became very
emotional. The sound of "Boolavogue" being played in these
surroundings was more than I could take, but the funny
thing about all of this was that the whole reception was
planned in a different way.

There was a full band of musicians waiting to play
"Boolavogue" when they saw the Wexford team coming
through the main exit, but I had come through a small side-
door and upset things a bit. It must have been fifteen
minutes before all the team and officials got through the
customs and were ready to emerge to the public area. During
those fifteen minutes, I got a foretaste of what this whole
experience was going to be like. People kept coming up to me
and telling me who they were, where they were originally
from, and where they had travelled from in the USA.

One man told me he had driven his car from San
Francisco, a journey of three thousand miles. For five years,

he had been saving money to take his family to where he was reared in County Wexford. He was in America for over thirty years, and the last surviving member of his family had died in Ireland earlier that year; he had no home to return to, so he decided to take his American wife and three grown-up children to New York to meet the Wexford team. They had all taken a month off work. I asked him how did he know we were coming to New York, and he said there was a "Wexford Men's Association" in San Francisco, of which he was a member, and they had been following the fortunes of our team for the past few years and he thought this was the nearest he would ever get to Wexford now.

Another man told me he had come down from Toronto, a journey of 650 miles. Many of the people standing around were members of the "Wexford Men's Association" in New York and, when I was thanking them for bringing us over to America, they said it was much cheaper to bring twenty fellows over from Ireland than it would be for all of them to fly to Ireland to see us play. Some of these people had been in the States for up to forty years, and their chance of every going back to their homeland was slim. They said no one would know them there now.

We were taken from the airport to Gaelic Park, where we were given a great reception and a good meal. Gaelic Park was owned by John (Kerry) O'Donnell and consisted of a fine playing field, a restaurant and bar, and a huge function room. Mr. O'Donnell seemed to control everything Irish in New York at that time. Later that evening we were taken to our hotel, which was the Henry Hudson Hotel, at 353 West 57 St. By New York standards, this hotel was not extra large, but to us it was huge. It was more than forty storeys high, and we each had our own room with bath, telephone, etc.. I had never used a telephone before then, and some of the other gadgets in the room confused me too. I was the only one of the team on the 29th floor.

Before we went to bed on that Friday night, we had a meeting and were informed of the few official engagements that we were all expected to attend. Nickey Rackard impressed on us the importance of winning the game against Cork on Sunday. The plan was to get a good sleep on that Friday night, take it easy on Saturday, get another good night's sleep and then beat Cork on Sunday. We would get a few dollars for pocket money on Monday, and then we were free to do as we pleased. Because of the heat, it was difficult enough to have a good night's sleep.

On that Saturday before the match, a few of us went for a stroll on the streets and we came to Jack Dempsey's place. Jack was the former world heavyweight boxing champion and we had our photograph taken with him and he signed some autographs. He seemed very interested in us when we told him who we were and what we were doing in New York, but, as we left the place, a very nice lady informed us that we

From left: Ned Wheeler, Jack Dempsey (former World Heavyweight Boxing Champion), Mick O'Hanlon and Tom Butler outside Jack Dempsey's restaurant in New York.

had spent twelve minutes with Mr. Dempsey and that would cost us $20, the photo would be extra. When we paid our bill and came outside, one of the lads remarked, "If we come across another one of these blokes, I'm only going to look in through the window at him."

Sunday, 2 June, was hot, it was very hot. There was no sunshine, just a clammy hot air that would do nothing for you when you breathed it into your lungs. It was almost unbearable on the coach, as we made our way through the traffic to the Polo Grounds. The atmosphere around the grounds was very different to Croke Park. There was very little colour, and that great Yankee drawl could be heard all around the place. As we collected our gear and headed into the stadium, people just stood and watched us. Some were shouting some kind of jargon they use at baseball games and American football games. I heard one smiling lady say, "I sure wouldn't mind if one of those boys called to ma door." We had a quick look at the pitch and, apart from the fact that one end was oval-shaped, it was fine. There was a nice bit of grass on it, and it wasn't too hard.

When the teams came out onto the park, the crowd reaction was very different to Croke Park. There were thirty four thousand fans there, but they didn't know what they were supposed to do. At first a few people started to clap their hands and, after a minute or so, everyone was clapping and cheering. I remember thinking, these people are not very enthusiastic about what they have come to see, but how wrong I was! As the teams lined up for the parade before the game, Jim (Tough) Barry, the famous Cork trainer, decided that he would march behind the band and lead the two teams. Jim was wearing a red hand-knitted polo-neck jumper, and how he could bear the heat, I'll never know. On the back of the jumper was the word, 'Cork', and on the front, 'Barry'. Because I had heard my mother sing the American

National Anthem so often, I was able to sing both Anthems as they were played, and I felt so proud.

Since the pitch was a bit small and the ball went out of play a lot, you couldn't say the game was a classic. The first half was very even, with the score at half time, Wexford 2-03, Cork 2-01. As the crowd got into the swing of things and those who had no previous knowledge of the game began to understand what it was all about, they gave great support to both teams. Wexford's team was the same as that which played in the All-Ireland Final. Tom Dixon got injured and was replaced at half time by Oliver Gough. Gough went centre forward and I took Tom's place, in at corner forward. Gradually, Wexford got on top and played some power-packed hurling as only they could do at the time. Oliver Gough was young and fresh, and played the best hurling he ever did for Wexford. The crowd got behind Wexford and you would think you were back in Croke Park. The final score was, Wexford 7-15, Cork 5-05. We had done what we had come to do, and we pleased those who had made sacrifices to bring us here.

We had ten days left to explore this whole new world and this new way of living that I had never even heard of. We had to turn down many invitations to visit people's homes. For the first time, I saw such things as escalators and lifts, freezers and refrigerators. When I remarked on how nice and tender my steak was one evening, I was told it was dead for at least six months. I can tell you, that didn't help my appetite one bit. I discovered, too, why New York is called the city that never sleeps. Between two and five o'clock in the morning the streets were buzzing with activity. All deliveries to the shops and hotels were carried out during these hours. The streets were cleaned and the garbage collected, and the speed and efficiency of the workers was very impressive.

One morning, a few of us were walking back to our hotel, when we noticed a man, single-handedly, unloading a lorry load of crates. There was a small platform on the back of his lorry and, on to this, he would put six crates, with his hand truck. He would then step onto the platform with his hand truck, and the platform would drop to ground level. He would unload the six crates, step back onto the platform, and up she would go again. To us this was one of the seven wonders of the world, but then we had never heard of hydraulics.

Some of what we saw and heard, I can remember well. We got an official welcome on the steps of City Hall, from the Mayor of New York, Mr. Robert Wagner. We met Cardinal Spellman, whose granny came from Kilbride, in County Carlow. We visited the US Military Academy and were taken on a boat-trip around Manhattan Island. We saw the Statue of Liberty, and were taken aboard an aircraft carrier. As we sailed beneath the great suspension bridge that crosses the Hudson River, it was explained to us that the bridge was suspended by thousands of strands of wire, all twisted together, and if the wire was unravelled, there would be enough to go one and half times around the world.

We went to the top of the Empire State Building which was the highest building in the world at that time. We were taken to the horse racing, and we saw the New York 'Giants' play 'Milwaukee' in Baseball; but one of the things I remember very well was the night we were taken to the professional boxing. There was no television in Wexford at that time, so we had never seen boxing. We had ringside seats and were offered pints of beer before the show started. The main event was a fight between Stefan Redl and Frank Hipolito. I think they were middleweights, and whoever won this fight would get a crack at the World Champion, so these fellows were pretty good. Before the big fight, there were three or four supporting bouts, and it was from these we got our night's entertainment. There was a heavyweight bout and a flyweight bout and a couple in between. These fellows all had flat noses and cauliflower ears. A lot of punches were thrown, but very few actually landed. Usually, the winner would come from behind and get a great cheer.

What made it funny for me was how the Wexford lads would take sides, with half of them cheering for one lad and the other half cheering for the other. Soon we had the big fanfare and all the glitter that goes with professional boxing, and these two very fine athletes began to destroy each other. It was cruel, it was bloody and it was wrong. There wasn't a word from the Wexford lads, and I think they were glad when it was over.

One morning about eleven o'clock I had nothing to do, so I went for a walk down Broadway to see the shops. I was looking in a shop window where there was some sportswear, and I glanced at a man standing very close beside me, who was looking into the window too. I got a mighty surprise because I knew who he was right away, but still, I was afraid I could be wrong, so I backed out behind him on the pavement to have a better view of him. There was another young lad with him and they both moved on down the street, and I followed them. When they stopped again to look in another window, I went up to him and said, "Are you Ronnie Delaney?" and he said "Yes". I told him who I was and what I was doing in New York, and he introduced me to his friend and said he was a Scot, and that they were running in an Athletic Meeting in New York that evening. Ronnie Delaney had won a Gold Medal for Ireland, a few months earlier, at the Olympic Games in Melbourne.

I spent two days with my long-lost wealthy cousins in Long Island, and got a close-up look at what life was like for a middle class family in New York at that time. They had a beautiful house with every modern convenience. Every member of the family was working, with the exception of one girl who was still at college, and each had their own car. Apart from the mother, who was my cousin, they showed very little interest in me or what I was doing in New York. It could be that I was there at a bad time for the family, but the impression I got was, they had very little time for anything other than their own interests.

On Sunday, 9 June, we played New York in Gaelic park and beat them, 3-10 to 2-06. Again, a fine crowd attended this game, with many of them Wexford people who had come to New York to spend the two weeks with the team. The Tyrone Football team played a New York selection before the hurling game, but could only muster thirteen players, so they asked if some of us Wexford lads would stand in until half time. Ted Morrissey and I volunteered to help them out; it was not a good idea. For a start, the pitch was rock hard, and they asked me to play at centre field. The New York lads were pretty tough, with the result that, more than my feet were sore by half time. I then had to play for Wexford in the second game, and the heat was unbearable. I got hit on the eyebrow and had to come off in the first half. A young doctor put two stitches in the wound, and I went on again for the second half, only to get hit again. This time I got one stitch on the top of my head and decided I'd had enough for one day.

The most enjoyable function we attended while in New York was the Official Reception given by the New York "Wexford Men's Association". This group of people had worked very hard for months, to make our trip possible. Most of them had been in New York for years, and we would not have known them. The one man I remember well is Mike Hynes, who was the driving force behind the whole venture. These people just couldn't do enough for us. We were presented with gold watches, and more than one man told me if I wanted to emigrate to America with my family at any time, they would be there to help me. Some of them knew in their hearts they would never go back to Ireland because their families had all died out. The number of people I met that night, who were reared within a ten mile radius of my home was unbelievable.

That night I learned about the good things, and the bad things, that emigration had done for the Irish people. A man by the name of O'Shea, from the parish of Davidstown, just outside of Enniscorthy, told me how he had been working for the farmers in the mid twenties when he got an opportunity to go to America. He packed his bags and came to the States without ever really saying goodbye. He thought he could go back if things didn't work out, but that wasn't to be. The first two or three years were difficult because he had to learn new skills and a whole new way of life. He told me how he had worked hard, with the intention that some day he would go back home, but instead he got married and had two daughters. He said all thoughts of ever going home had to be abandoned now, so he stuffed them into a black hole somewhere in his heart. "But what I have seen here tonight" he said, "has blown that hole wide open again." He had become very emotional now and his younger daughter, who had just finished college and was with him that night, put

Part of the attendance at the Official Reception given by the New York Wexford Mens Association.

her arms around him and said, "Dad, you sentimental old fool!" She didn't understand, but then, how could she?

We left New York for home on 13 June. It was mid afternoon, and the heat was unbearable as we made our way across the tarmac to board the plane. We had been told there was a heat wave on the way, and we were glad to be leaving. As we settled in our seats, we were informed that the plane was making its maiden flight across the Atlantic, and I heard one of the lads say he hoped whoever made it tightened up all the nuts and screws. I have never felt so tired and exhausted as I did when I took an inside seat by a window, just behind the left wing of the plane. Again, we were reminded that we would be flying back through the night and the hours of darkness would be few. The journey would be direct and would take about nine hours. I thought to myself, "I'll be asleep, so it doesn't matter how long it takes." But how wrong I was!

As soon as the pilot started the engines and pulled out onto the runway, you didn't have to be an expert to notice the difference between this plane and the one that had taken us to the States. This one was very silent, compared to the other one and appeared to have a lot more power. As she rose, like a giant bird, and turned towards the Atlantic Ocean, I was looking down on this great city that we were leaving behind. As we climbed higher into the sky, the streets and motorways became narrower and people and cars became tiny, like ants running in all directions. Years later, when I first heard the words 'rat race' used, my mind took me back to the scene that was underneath us now. In places, there were six and eight lanes of traffic on the motorways, and, on the sidewalks, people travelling at speed brushed shoulders, but never made eye contact. We had spent sixteen hectic days in that mighty city and I had enjoyed it immensely, but I saw nothing that would make me want to come back.

It was only a matter of minutes until we were out over the Atlantic and all that was to be seen below us was water, so I turned my attention to what was taking place on the plane. After a short while we were offered some refreshments and there was lots of noise and movement for two or three hours and then, suddenly, we were flying into the night. The lights in the plane were dimmed and the place became quiet and people began to fall asleep. I, too, tried to sleep, but without much success. As the night grew very dark, I could see flames coming from the exhaust pipes on my side of the plane. As I was sitting close to the wing, this was frightening at times. The only sound now was the continuous drone of the engines, and my mind began to wander back over the past two weeks.

We had come to New York to play hurling, and this we had done very well. We had brought great joy to all those people who had come from all over the States to see us play, and that gave us great satisfaction. We heard great success stories from the hundreds of Wexford people who had emigrated to America in the past forty years and more, but I saw and heard a lot that made me sad, and disappointed too. I didn't feel sleepy anymore, and my mind went into overdrive as I stared out of the window. The sky had become clear and I could see the sea glistening way down below us. As the moon was on the south side of the plane, and I was looking north, I couldn't see it, but I could see its reflection on the water. We were in the air now for about four or five hours, so I came to the conclusion we were a thousand miles from land. Looking out the window, you wouldn't know we were moving. It looked as if we were standing in space.

I thought of the stories my mother told me about her journey to Ireland in 1908, when she was a thirteen year old child. Because her parents had died, she was sent from America to Ireland, to be reared by her aunt. The only transport across the Atlantic at that time was by boat, and the boat on which she travelled took weeks to make the crossing. To her dying day she said she could smell the filth and sickness in the boat. I would make the crossing in nine hours. What progress had been made in fifty years!

Other things that were going through my mind, as I stared into space, were the stories I was told by men who had to leave Ireland during the Civil War. It was now thirty five years since these men were forced to leave their homes. One man was from the same parish as myself, and he told me how he was taken to Cobh by five men and put on a boat and told never to come home. One of these men was his own brother, a man I knew very well. Another man I met was a member of a family I also knew very well, but when I came home and told these people I had met their brother, they told me never to mention his name to anyone again. I thought, too, of all the fine people I had met, who made us so welcome and brought us to their homes and gave us presents to take home. When I got home, I had a lot more money than I had brought with me. People actually shoved money into our pockets.

For two hours more, my mind kept churning through the strange things that I had seen and heard in the past sixteen days. I suppose what amazed me most, was how wealthy people seemed to be and how advanced they were, technically. We, here in Ireland, were living in a different world back then; but we have caught up with them in the past few years. The most harrowing experience we had in New York was on the day we were brought on a bus tour of Harlem. We were told that the windows of the bus were bullet-proof, and that the bus would not be stopping. I had never heard of Harlem, and I couldn't understand what all the fuss was about. Every time I see pictures on the telly of black starving people in Ethiopia and all those other African countries, it reminds me of what I saw in Harlem. The sun was very hot on the day we passed through the place, and the children were sitting on the pavement. Men were standing in groups and the women were looking out the doors as we passed through. It was hard to believe that such poverty and squalor was allowed to exist in a city that displayed such wealth.

When I looked at my watch now, I discovered we were more than seven hours in the air, so I went about changing my watch to Irish time, but my brain was so tired I hadn't a clue what time it should be, so I just set it at five o'clock. All of a sudden, my thoughts turned to home and to Kitty and the children. We were flying into the dawn, now, and I could see the lovely brightness ahead of us.

I felt tired and sore, but wide awake. I had two very sore knuckles on my left hand with lumps of skin missing, two stitches in my left eyebrow and one on top of my head. Those were the only stitches I got in twenty two years of hurling, but the skinned knuckles were an every-day occurrence. Very quickly we were into full daylight, and I was looking below for the first sign of land. Soon, the sound of the engines being cut down and that sinking feeling you get in your stomach told us we were near the end of our great adventure. Small pieces of fluffy white cloud were interrupting my view as I watched for the first sight of land. We were informed that the time was 6.20am, Irish time, and I went to adjust my watch. When I glanced out the window again, I could see the jagged coastline of Clare and I became a bit emotional. I thanked God for our safe return, and I thanked Him too for the game of hurling.

I end this story here, with our return from the trip to New York. The reason I do so is because that particular panel of players who made the breakthrough in the '50s never played together again. Bobby Rackard had a bad accident on his farm two weeks after our return and was forced to retire from inter-county hurling. Nickey Rackard retired after we were beaten in the 1957 Leinster Championship. Many of us continued playing and we won the '57-'58 National League. Billy Rackard, Nick O'Donnell, Jim English, Jim Morrissey, Mick Morrissey, Ned Wheeler, Seamus Hearne, Harry O'Connor, Padge Kehoe, Oliver Gough, Tim Flood and I all played in that final.

In 1960, Nick O'Donnell, Jim English, Billy Rackard, Ned Wheeler, Jim Morrissey, Padge Kehoe, Tim Flood and I got our third All-Ireland medal in the space of six years. Of the players who made the breakthrough in the '50s, the last two survivors to play in an All-Ireland final were Ned Wheeler and myself when we were beaten by Tipperary in the 1965 final.

I sometimes wonder what my life would have been like if I had never taken a hurl in my hand. From the age of six, I could swing a hurl well, and carried one with me almost everywhere I went. Growing up on a farm and walking three miles to school, there were many ways to use a hurl. Without ever noticing it, the hurl became like an extra limb, or an extension to my arms. Until I was fourteen years old, I never played a real hurling match, but learned to protect myself and survive in the rough and tumble of the school hurling pitch.

My first ambition was to play for the club minor team and then, with a bit of luck, for the senior team, but winning anything at inter-county level was out of the question. By the time I was eighteen I began to dream of great games and great occasions; the dream continues and I know it will never end until I draw my last breath. Still, at seventy five years of age, I sometimes take a nice well balanced hurl in my hand and a crisp white hurling ball and get the urge to belt the ball ninety yards. It's like being introduced to a nice good looking young girl; it's a romance, and you wish you were young again.

One night, after I had sung a few songs at a concert in Enniscorthy, a young woman came up to me and said, "Why don't you, or someone like you, write the story of that Wexford team of the '50s?" She said she had an uncle who never stopped talking about that team, even on his death bed. It was then I decided to tell the story - *The Way I Saw It*.

Several times each year I attend games in Croke Park and marvel at the improvements and changes that have taken place there since I last hurled on its sod. Last summer I was told by a friend that if I went there mid-week I could be taken on a guided tour of the place so, making use of my 'free travel pass', I arrived in Croke Park about 11 o' clock one Thursday and was informed by a man that he would be taking a group of people on tour at 12.30. He told us we would see every nook and cranny of this very modern sports facility and that the tour would take about two hours. After we climbed up to the press box and the commentary position, my legs were telling me I needed to rest, so I let the party move on and I sat down in one of the pressmen's seats. The view was magnificent but I thought it a bit unreal. The place was very quiet and the only living things I could see were a few seagulls resting in the middle of the pitch. I sat there for a few minutes to get my breath back, and my mind began to wander.

When a person is as old as I am now, simple things get your mind racing back over the years. To be in Croke Park on the day your county wins its first All-Ireland, or wins one after a break of twenty-five years or more, is the nearest thing to heaven you will ever experience on this earth. I was here to see Galway, Offaly, Clare and Wexford win such hurling All Irelands. I've seen Down, Derry, Donegal, Armagh and Tyrone win their first football All-Irelands and I felt privileged to be there. Dreams come true for men and women on All Ireland Final days, days they thought they might never see. I was lucky enough to be part of a Wexford team that won a couple of All Irelands here. I've also felt the deep disappointment that can only be experienced when playing for the losing side on All Ireland day.

As I sat there now looking around this empty stadium, I thought to myself: why do people get so worked up and excited about a game of hurling or football? As a neutral supporter I've sat in my seat in the stand watching men and women cry, while others run on to the pitch and go down on their knees to kiss the ground. There is no monetary reward for these people. They return to their homes and the only things they have gained are memories, memories that will remain with them until the day they die. The GAA has given us a sense of pride in our place and a feeling of belonging. Fifty years have brought great changes to the structure that is Croke Park, but the atmosphere in the place on Final day hasn't changed.

I moved from the press box to the commentary position and I thought of Michael O'Hehir's great commentaries in the Forties and Fifties. On the breeze I caught the lilting voice of Micheál Ó Muircheartaigh as he describes the scene in his own inimitable way. These men have done more than their share to popularise our games, and, I thought, what about the 'foot-soldiers' of the GAA? They really, are the people who built the GAA and Croke Park and we must never forget them. Most of them are unknown outside their own club and parish, but they have given a lifetime of service to our games. One such person that comes to mind is Mikie Redmond from my own club, Rathnure. I mention him as an example and there are people like Mikie in every club around the country. As a twelve year old boy, he was one of eight people who, in 1931, met to form the hurling club. Ever since, he has played a major part in building the club to what it is today. He was an outstanding player and a great administrator. Today at 86 years of age, he is Honorary President of the Club that he worked so hard to build.

My mind was full of memories as I reluctantly left the commentary box to make my way back down to ground level. Certainly what I saw on the tour impressed me and I would recommend that every person with an interest in the GAA visit Croke Park and take this guided tour. I felt that in a very small way I too, like thousands of others, had done something to build this magnificent stadium. I stopped a few times, trying to visualise what the place was like when I first set foot here with my cobbled boots tied around my hurl, fifty five years ago.

Memories, memories and more memories.

All-Ireland Final Team with all trophies won in 1956 - All-Ireland, Leinster Championship, National League, Oireachtas and Walsh Cup. Back row: Billy Rackard, Martin Codd, Bobby Rackard, Tom Ryan, Ned Wheeler, Nick O'Donnell, Jim Morrissey, Nickey Rackard, front row: Tom Dixon, Padge Kehoe, Mick Morrissey, Jim English, Art Foley, Seamus Hearne. (Tim Flood is missing).

Tim Flood and myself, always good friends.

Michéal O'Hehir, whose contribution to the advancement of the GAA in the '40s and '50s was immense. With his very distinct voice and his knowledge of the games he brought all the excitement and passion of the games to the four corners of Ireland. It was his radio commentary that made all the great players household names all over the country.

Ned Wheeler and myself (the last survivors of the early '50's) do battle with the great John Doyle of Tipperary in the All-Ireland Final of 1965. The Wexford player on the right is Joe Foley.

This is me fifty years ago. The only change is the hair style.

Presentation of trophies in Rathnure in 1955 (from left to right): Martin Codd, Nickey Rackard, Dr. Paddy Daly, Jim English, Billy Rackard, Bobby Rackard and Fr. Doyle P.P.

**Bobby Rackard showing all his great power.
When the stakes were high Bobby would go that extra mile.**

**Ted Bolger on the left, played many games for Wexford in
the good years.**

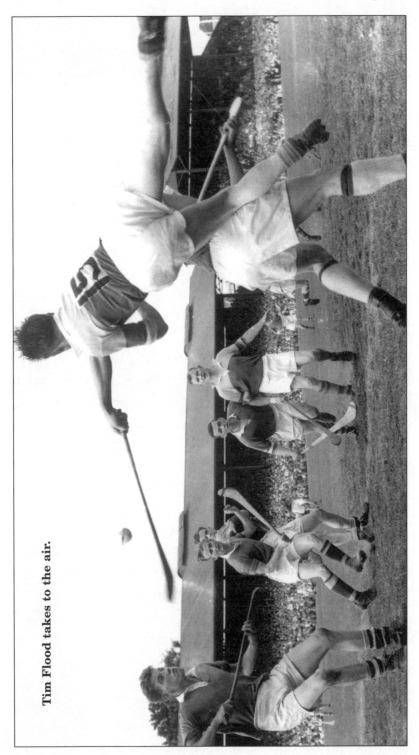

Tim Flood takes to the air.

PROFILES

ART FOLEY

Art Foley makes another fine save. No special goalie's hurl in those days.

Art Foley was small for a goalkeeper. He was of stocky build and very strong. He had long arms and a huge pair of safe hands. He walked with long steps and stood with his feet well apart. When he got a grip on a ball it was very hard to stop him hitting it. In the early years he didn't seem to have great confidence in himself or perhaps not a lot of interest at inter-county level, but when Nick O'Donnell came to Enniscorthy and started to play fullback for St Aidan's they became a great combination for club and county. Much has been said and written about Art's famous save from Christy Ring in the 1956 All-Ireland final and with the passing years the stories get better. Ring was going straight for his ninth All- Ireland senior hurling medal and time was running out with Wexford gone into a two point lead and just three minutes to go. Christy got this breaking ball and for the first time in the game he got clean away from Bobby Rackard and headed straight for goal. Now, many times Cork people had seen Ring destroy the opposition with one burst like this near the end of a big game and this looked like it was going to be his greatest goal. Every Cork man and woman in the stands was on their feet by the time Ring let go a fierce drive from just 21 yards and what happened in the next ten seconds has been told in many different ways. But now after 49 years, I can tell the truth as it has been told to me by three different people who were behind Art's goal on the day and better still by Art himself. I wrote to Art in America where he has been living for over forty years, just to get the truth about the famous save, and the following is Art's version of events:

"Well Martin to get down to Basics about the "save," I sometimes wonder if it really happened or was it just my imagination, time has passed so fast & the story has lost nothing" the telling. My memories of that day are still fresh in my mind. I can still see the events leading up to & including the save. Christy had gotten very Restless when we went two points up & Roamed outfield from the corner. He was about forty yards out to my left under the Long Stand side of the field, when he grabbed a clearance from the Cork backline. He immediately took off on a solo Run straight down the field & then cut across to the Cusack Stand side. He was being pursued by Jim Morrissey & Billy, he then cut back to the Long Stand side of the field with the Remainder of the Back line in pursuit, as I watched things unfold & the 54' Final flashed into my mind especially Johnny Clifford's Goal we gave Cork a gift that day, but I vowed to myself not to-day. Christy was still in motion & by now was on the 21 yard line when he let fly for what he thought was the winning goal. I will now digress for a moment. Everybody in Croke Park talked about the catch I made, I did not catch that ball, I blocked the ball with my Hurley, the ball went

straight up in the air. I glanced outfield & spotted
Hartnett & Murphy thundering in like two Sherman
Tanks, I said 'Oh God I'm Dead,' I decided to block the
ball out, if I had caught it I would have been buried
in the goal ball & all. I spotted Jim Morrissey out to
my left & blocked the ball in his direction, as I got
rid of the ball, I was buried in the left corner of the
net. I was lying there with the two of them on top of
me when the ball struck the outside of the net for a
moment my heart stopped I thought they scored, until
I saw John Keane the umpire signal wide.

New Martin all this action was like
a camera shoot, everything clicking, in sequence. When
we got extricated from the net, Christy came rushing
in grabbed me by the hair & said you little Black Bastard
you have beaten us, he then shook hands & congratulated
me. I replied it is about so & so time someone did. The
subsequent puck out by Nicko was cleared by the Cork
Back Line & Pat Dowling sent in a high dropping ball
into the goalmouth, I caught & cleared to Seamus
at mid-field he passed onto Tom Ryan & Tom to Nicky
& Croke Park exploded when Nick scored from 35 yards
out. Well Martin those are my memories of that great
day for Wexford Hurling & it was an honor & a privilege
to have been a member of the greatest team ever to
win the All-Ireland.

                                   Art Foley.

BOBBY RACKARD

If I was asked who was my favourite player from the
Wexford team of the fifties I'd have no hesitation in saying it
was Bobby Rackard. Apart altogether from hurling, I
admired Bobby greatly. We attended school together in
Rathnure and we never moved away from the locality. Bobby
was the middle child in a family of nine. I was in the middle

An injured and tattered Tom Dixon in the Polo Grounds, New York, with Mick O'Hanlon and Tom Butler on his left.

Bobby Rackard in New York, a shy and private man.

Enjoying the sun in New York - seated from left: Ted Morrissey, Ned Wheeler, Billy Rackard, Bobby Rackard (partially hidden), Tom Dixon, Seamus Hearne and Nickey Rackard.

The following five pages contain photographs taken at a get-together in Rackard's of Killanne in September 1988. Eighteen members of the 1950s panel were present at the function. Some of the players hadn't met for over 30 years.

Martin Flood, Dom Hearne, Mick Morrissey, Martin Byrne, Martin Codd, Tim Flood, Ted Morrissey.

Mick Morrissey, Betty Rackard and Ted Morrissey.

Bobby Rackard, Tom Dixon, Mick Morrissey.

Jim English, Jim Morrissey, Mick Morrissey, Ted Morrissey
and Dom Hearne.

**Tom Dixon, Ned Wheeler, Artie Foley, Tom Ryan, Billy Kielthy,
Bobby Donovan.**

**Padge Kehoe (right) with his life-long friend Jimmy Kavanagh
who was always in the dressing room to give advice.**

Martin Codd, Jim Morrissey and Bobby Rackard.

Billy Kielthy, Artie Foley and Martin Flood.

**Wilkie bursts into song despite the best efforts of Billy Rackard
to restrain him!**

**Attending the 1798 celebration in The Shannon on
St. Patrick's Day 1998 were: Tom Ryan, Ted Morrissey,
Wilkie Thorpe and Harry O'Connor.**

Bobby Rackard.

of seven. We both married young and had large families. We both inherited the family home and business which left us with a lot of responsibility at a young age. We neither smoked nor drank alcohol which was a help to our hurling careers. While at school we were the organisers of the lunchtime hurling match. While sitting in the back desk we would check who was in school and who was missing and then pick our teams and be ready to go as soon as the bell would ring. We would play on each other at centre-field and give the instructions to our respective teams from there. There were times when our playing pitch was a stubble field. As a boy, Bobby was tall but very light, with a fragile appearance. By the age of twenty he had changed to a giant of a man with powerful arms and shoulders. As hurlers go, Bobby could never be described as a purest. He was a once off who learned his trade the hard way. In the early '40's when Bobby was in his early teens a group of men and boys would congregate in the Barrack field in Killanne every summer evening and Sunday afternoons to play hurling. The Barrack field was so called because it was behind the Garda Barracks in Killanne. It was part of Rackards farm and was always nice and bare, as it was grazed by horses. Most of these lads were not serious hurling students; they were just there for the fun. Few would have hurling boots or togs and their hurls would be home made and heavy. Speed would not be a big part of the game as most of the participants would be wearing their work boots and clothes. What Bobby learned here, was how to survive and look after himself at fifteen years of age. By the time he was eighteen there was no more he could learn in the

Barrack field so he moved to greener pastures. He was never known to leave the field of play through injury but he missed all of '53 when a simple operation went very wrong. While playing his best hurling at 30 years of age his hurling career was ended by a tragic farm accident.

Bobby's display in the second half of the All Ireland final of '54 was the greatest exhibition of defending ever seen and those who saw it were privileged. His brilliant displays throughout the fifties earned him a place on the 'Team of the Millennium'.

NICK O'DONNELL

Nick O'Donnell was born just outside Graiguenamanagh in Co. Kilkenny and came to live in Enniscorthy in 1950. He had won a junior All Ireland with Kilkenny in 1946 and was a sub on their senior team in 1947, when they won the senior championship. How he was let slip through the net by the Kilkenny selectors is still a mystery. Soon after he arrived in Enniscorthy he was playing at full-back for the St Aidan's club. If Nick O' Donnell had come to live in some

Nick O'Donnell waiting to receive the McCarthy Cup from Dr. Stewart, the President of the G.A.A. in 1960.

other part of Co Wexford he might have been lost to hurling forever. There were some shrewd hurling brains in the St Aidan's club and they knew immediately they had someone special. Nicko played full-back for Wexford for eleven years and won every honour in the game. He was captain of the team when we won the All Ireland in '55 and again in 1960. Because he was a great ball player and a great reader of the game he would still be a great full-back in today's game. Off the field of play he was shy and retiring and never one to seek special attention. He was unique as a full-back because he always took the puck out from goal. This was because he had a mighty puck on the ball. I doubt if there will ever be a better full-back than Nick O'Donnell. He was selected at full-back on the 'Team of the Millennium'.

MICK MORRISSEY

I first saw Mick Morrissey when he played for his home club, St Mullins who were then Carlow County champions. The game was just a challenge match and was between Rathnure and St Mullins and was played in Rathnure. Being ajoining parishes we would play these games now and again just for a bit of practice. We were Wexford county champions at the time and were considered a bit better than St Mullins,

Mick Morrissey with the ball in his hand, comes out to make a vital clearance in the All-Ireland Final of 1956. He is surrounded by some of the game's greatest-ever players. On the ground is Paddy Barry who seems to have tripped Christy Ring. Bobby Rackard, Josie Hartnett and Nick O'Donnell are the other players closeby.

but this one young lad who was about eighteen, was hurling in a gear way above anyone else on the field, so I asked someone who he was. I was told he was a Morrissey of Ballycrinnigan. He did look a bit special but I heard no more about him for a while until he began working in New Ross and decided to play for the club there. In 1954 he played for the Wexford Junior team and was brought into the senior panel early in 1955. He was very ambitious and every chance he got he made full use of it. Every game he played he gave one hundred percent. He was a good two handed hurler and approached the game in a very professional way. He had a number of brothers who were all good hurlers. Mick got his big break when he was selected at wing back for the Leinster final against Kilkenny in 1955. It was his first competitive game for Wexford at senior level. To add to the challenge, he would be marking one of the most stylish players ever to put on a Kilkenny jersey, Sean Clohessy, who had everything we expect in a Kilkenny hurler. After a shaky start Mick took complete control of the situation and played a blinder. He became the final link in a chain that for two years was unbreakable. He later emigrated to New York, where he became a very successful businessman.

JIM ENGLISH

Jim English from Rathnure came on as a sub at wing back

in the Leinster final of 1953. He had been in the subs for two years but never got much of a chance to prove his worth. He was young and not very big but when he got his opportunity he never looked back. He played in the same position for ten years and only once can I remember him being replaced, which was when he was

Jim English.

badly injured in the 1956 league final. Seldom if ever did he have a poor game and most times he was brilliant. He was the only member of the team who held the hurl with the left hand on the top. Jim was a bit like a cat, you just couldn't knock him off his feet. I saw men two or three stone heavier bang into him, but only his hand would hit the ground. Jim's work rate was exceptional and he was always available for a pass. He had a great understanding with Bobby Rackard and Nick O'Donnell. This was before the rules were changed and you could drop the hurl and hand-pass the ball. Bobby Rackard was an expert at this and Jim was always there to take the pass. Often when a high ball was dropping in near the goal and Nicko thought it too risky to try catch it he would "bat" it out to the wing where Jim always seemed to be waiting. I often heard it said after a game that Jim English had hit more balls than any other player on the field. He was captain of the team in 1956.

BILLY RACKARD

Billy Rackard, the youngest of the three famous brothers, was a slow starter at inter-county level. He had a few set backs as a boy, which left him weak and a bit slow to develop his skills. He first came on the team as a corner back late in 1949 but didn't make a big impression. He looked slow but could handle the ball well so because the selectors saw his potential they persevered with him. Being an intelligent and proud man Billy worked hard on his game and

Billie Rackard, a powerful athlete at the pinnacle of his career.

slowly but surely he became a powerful athlete, standing six feet tall and weighing about thirteen and a half stone. He moved to centre back in 1955, a position he held for the remainder of his career. He perfected the art of catching the dropping ball as he held off his opponent with his shoulder, protecting his hand with his hurl. He had many majestic performances, was very flamboyant and always the best dressed man in the squad.

JIM MORRISSEY

One of a large family of hurlers, footballers and camogie players from Camross in the heart of county Wexford, Jim Morrissey came onto the Wexford hurling team late in 1949. A fraction short of six feet tall and weighing fourteen stone, Jim was a very strong man and knew how to use his weight and strength. Though always relaxed and good humoured and a very clean hurler, he always gave the impression that if there was trouble he could look after himself. Most of his hurling was done at centre field, but he had a few outstanding games in the half back line too. Left or right, in the air, on the ground or from the hand, it was all the same to Jim. His hits were solid and long, but never wild. His line cuts would usually drop in around the square but never wide. In his own quiet way he was always encouraging his team-mates, and he seldom gave away a free. He had a unique way of hitting with

Jim Morrissey, a very solid and consistently good player.

the hip, a hit that left his opponents stunned for a minute or two. He had a long and successful career and gave great pleasure to the faithful Wexford supporters.

SEAMUS HEARNE

When Seamus Hearne first appeared in a Wexford jersey he was playing at corner back. This game against Meath was the first round of the Leinster championship in 1950. I thought he was as bad a corner back as I had ever seen and that we would never see him again playing for the county. How wrong I was and how good that

Seamus Hearne was Wexford's best player in the finals of 1955 and '56.

others didn't see him as I did! One thing I do remember is that when we were training no one liked playing on Seamus because although he might not be doing much himself, he was always in your way. The selectors kept playing Seamus on and off at corner-back but the position didn't suit his style at all. When moved to centre field in 1954 he suddenly became a different player and when in full flow he was a sight to see. He had a bow-legged run and always had the socks down around his ankles. He was always on the move and the longer the game went on, the faster he seemed to go. He had a unique way of hooking, and opponents who got to know his style were in dread of this. Instead of just holding his hurl out straight as most players did when hooking, Seamus would hold his hurl in both hands and with an upward jerk pull you hurl from your hands or your arms from their sockets. He and Billie Rackard were great pals and it was not unusual to see them both in the corner of the dressing room at half time during big games with Billy urging Seamus to greater effort. Especially on a hot summer's day, Seamus would lose more sweat than any player I have ever seen and to counteract this I often saw him put a thick smear of Vaseline over his eyebrows and down his cheeks. He said this kept the salt in the sweat from stinging his eyes. He was impossible to categorise, but what ever he was, he was Wexford's best player in the finals of '55 and '56.

NED WHEELER

Ned Wheeler.

One evening after training in Rathnure I was talking to a great old hurling man who was excited about a young lad he had seen playing minor for St Martin's the Sunday before. He described him as being a six-footer, very thin, with short bristly white hair. He seldom picked the ball but could strike left and right at top speed and would go through a stone wall. When he came near the sideline he said you could hear the swish of the hurl every time he hit the ball. This, of course, was Ned Wheeler who came on to the Wexford Senior hurling team in 1950 while still a minor. He always gave the impression when in full flight that he would sweep man, ball and all before him. He was also a good over-head striker and his best position was centre field. For a year or two he was light for his height and lacked stamina, but when he put on a couple of stone weight he was awesome. Ned was always a great man for the crack and had a fine singing voice. When we were on our way to New York in 1957 the plane touched down at Gander airport in Newfoundland to change planes or refuel, I can't remember which. We were all waiting around with our bags and hurls and people were throwing great looks at us, and an old American lady said to Wheeler, "I say, young man, what are these weapons you are carrying?" And in a flash, Ned said, "Billhooks Ma'am". "I beg your pardon," she said. "Billhooks, Ma'am, Billhooks, we play hurling with them. It's a field game something like hockey, but much rougher". "Oh dear," she said, "but why do you have two hooks?" "Ah sure, Ma'am," said Ned, "some fellows play it very rough and might break a hook and then they need a replacement". One of the selectors was standing a bit away and he had 12 hurls that he was taking to a friend in New York, and an old lady was heard to say to her companion, "Gee, Ester, he sure must be a real rough player". Her friend looked at him over her specks and said, "He looks like one of the mafia". Ned Wheeler was born in Rathdowney in County Laois and came to Wexford at a young age. He first played for St Martin's, Piercestown, but finished his hurling career with Faythe Harriers.

PADGE KEHOE

Padge Kehoe had every skill there is in the game of hurling. He also had the speed and brains to put these skills to full use. Some would say Padge lacked aggression, but having played against him many times in club games I would see him in a different way. Some players have too much aggression for their own good. I once heard Bobby

Padge Kehoe.

Rackard say that he used to go out of his way to shoulder fellows until he discovered that it was best to avoid physical contact unless it was necessary. I think Padge too got this one just about right. He put on the Wexford jersey more times than any other player in the history of the game and, after Nicky Rackard, he had most influence on his team mates. The famous St Aidan's Club in Enniscorthy was built around Padge Kehoe and they won ten county championships in the short period of their existence. Born and reared on a farm just a mile outside Enniscorthy, he is a son of Padraig Kehoe who was a well known public figure.

TIM FLOOD

Tim Flood keeps his eye on the ball.

Like most rural clubs, when Cloughbawn burst on the scene as a force in senior hurling in the late '40s, they were backboned by five sets of brothers. Of these the Floods became the most prominent. Martin and Tim were brothers. They were first cousins of Sean and Gerry who were also brothers. Martin and Sean played many games both in the League and championship for the County in the early '50s but could never hold a permanent position. Tim had no such problem. He first got a run with the county team in or around 1947 but was taken off at half time. If Cloughbawn had not got into senior hurling would Tim Flood never have had a platform to display his skills? After Cloughbawn won the county Championship in 1949, Tim came onto the county team and remained there for twelve years until he decided to retire. He played more times for Wexford in the '50s than any other man, with the exception perhaps of Billy Rackard. He won every honour in the game and in 1956 he played competitive games every Sunday for twenty six weeks. There is no end to the number of skills in the game of hurling and Tim mastered more of them than any other member of our team. He had speed and strength and know how to use both. He was a fierce competitor and a skilled tackler. He had a great sidestep but could take fellows on too. You never knew if he was going to juggle with the ball or play it straight. At five feet nine inches tall and weighing less than thirteen stone, he was one of the smallest players we had, but I cannot once remember him going off injured. He was a super star in the '50s and with his skills, if he was playing under today's rules he would be even better.

TOM RYAN

Tom Ryan was a Kilkenny man who came to work in Enniscorthy in the early '50s. He was in his mid-twenties and already a seasoned and battle-hardened hurler but he was no stylist. Like Nick O'Donnell he joined the St Aidan's club and soon became a vital member of their great teams. I don't know what category of forward you would

A relaxed Tom Ryan.

cast him in, but whatever it is he was very effective. There was no doubting his intelligence but you could question his tactics at times. Much of his misbehaving was done to take the backs' attention off his more skilful team-mates. He had a great knack of shielding and holding the ball when he got it near the gaol and would seldom hit a ball wide. He scored lots of goals and made many more. His inter-county career was short but sweet. He was a good friend and what you might describe as a 'likeable rogue'.

NICKEY RACKARD

From the time I was six years old Nickey Rackard was my hero. He was seven years older than me, and I often saw him when he was 12 or 13 years old, pass by our gateway on a huge horse. He would be blowing the hunting horn as he searched for foxhounds that had strayed from the pack a day of two before. The Bree Hounds were at that time in kennels at Coolbawn House near our home. On the very first day that I went to school in Rathnure, Nickey told me what to do when we played hurling at lunch-time. Twenty years later he was still telling me what to do, only now we were in Croke Park. Nickey's parents decided to send him to secondary school in

**Padge Kehoe and Nickey Rackard with the Leinster Cup.
Two great leaders of men.**

St Kieran's College, Kilkenny, and it was there that the dream began. From playing with and mixing with hurling people in that great nursery of the game, he developed a passion for hurling that was immense and by his example it has passed on to thousands of boys and girls in Wexford. It is impossible to say something about Nickey that has not already been said, but there is one thing of which I am very sure. No person ever had such an influence on a team as he had on the Wexford team of the '50s, and by his example he made us one of the most sporting and popular teams ever to play in Croke Park. In the space of ten years the Rathnure club and St Aidan's club of Enniscorthy played each other in six County finals. More than half of the county team at that time came from these two clubs and not once was there spite or animosity amongst the players. This was brought about by the example and leadership of Padge Kehoe and Nickey Rackard

TOM DIXON

As a member of St Aidan's hurling club in Enniscorthy, Tom Dixon won 7 county senior hurling championships in the '50s. He joined the county senior panel in 1952, but found it difficult to hold a permanent position early on. He was quiet and unobtrusive, and this more than any lack of hurling ability kept him in the subs for too

Tom Dixon.

long. He was very skilful but would never over-play the ball. After playing in many games and in many different positions, Tom got his big chance in 1956 when he was selected to play against Cork in a game that would decide who would play Tipperary in the National League final. Wexford won and Tom held his place at corner forward for the never-to-be-forgotten League final of 1956. He scored two vital goals in the second half of that game as Wexford came from being fifteen points down to win by four points. That same year in the All-Ireland final, Tom Dixon was again one of the stars and a nicer fellow you wouldn't meet.

PADDY KEHOE

I have still to see a man who can play both football and hurling better than Paddy Kehoe of Gusserawn. One of the older members of the hurling team of the '50s, Paddy had won a Leinster football championship with Wexford in 1945. On his day in either football or hurling Paddy was

Paddy Kehoe.   unstoppable. He was built like a tank and had great speed and skill. If today's training facilities had been available in the '50s he would have been one of the greatest players of all time. He always carried a little too much weight.

TED MORRISSEY

Ted Morrissey was a very fine hurler and it was a shame he spent so much of his time on the subs bench. He was a natural centre half back and his only failing was he was not as good as Bobby or Billy Rackard. A younger brother of Jim and he too started his career in Camross. He later went to work in

Enniscorthy and did all his club hurling with   **Ted Morrissey.**
St Aidan's, winning six or seven county championships.

BILLY WICKHAM

Nick O'Donnell's understudy throughout the good years, Billy Wickham was a fine fullback and gave some great displays when called upon. His best hour was against

Billy Wickham.

Tipperary in the National League final of 1955 when he replaced Billie Rackard who was unavailable. Whatever chance a forward had of going around Billy, he had no chance of going through him. He liked to play the game hard and enjoyed a good battle.

DOMINIC HEARN

Dominic Hearn of Horeswood was on the Wexford team for the 1949/50 National League campaign and was still thereabouts when they made the big break-through in 1955. He could never command a permanent place on the team but always played well when called upon. He played at centre field for his club and could more than hold his own against the best in the county in that position. He never got the chance to play centre field for Wexford but played in the forwards on many of the big occasions and only twelve of the "famous twenty-two" played more

Dominic Hearne in action against Kilkenny.

games for the county. I will always remember him as a loyal friend and perfect gentleman.

MICK O'HANLON

Mick O'Hanlon was twenty-seven or eight when he came onto the County hurling team. He had been playing with the football team for a number of years, so he had some

Mick O'Hanlon.

experience of the big occasion. While in St Peter's College, Wexford as a student, he had broken his left wrist practising high jump. This left him with a badly damaged wrist and it was miraculous that he could play hurling at all. Mick was what you would call a no-nonsense corner back. When you played on Mick O'Hanlon you knew you had been in a game. He always played fairly but could hit very hard. His speciality was the half forward coming in on a solo run. While Wexford were training for the All-Ireland semi-final in 1955 against Limerick, one of the press men came into the dressing-room one evening after training, looking for comments from the players. This Limerick team were very fast, so much so, that the press were referring to them as Mick Mackey's greyhounds. This reporter asked the question, "How will your backs cope with the speed of the Limerick forwards?" There was silence for a minute as we considered the question, then Mick cleared his throat and said, "Wouldn't it be a hoor to be going at that speed and run into something!" The reporter didn't print the comment but I think he got the message.

SAM 'WILKIE' THORPE

Born and reared on the slopes of the famous Vinegar Hill in Enniscorthy, Sam Thorpe was one of the unlucky few who did so much to build this great Wexford team, only to run out of time and get no All-Ireland medal. An outstanding footballer and hurler, always one for the crack and the witty remark, he had a relaxing effect on

Sam 'Wilkie' Thorpe.

everyone in the dressing-room, no matter how important the game was.

TIM RUSSELL

Even though he got no All-Ireland medal with Wexford, Tim Russell played a huge part in the success of our team in the '50s. Tim was born and reared in Doneraile, Co. Cork, and played a few games for Cork. He came to work in New Ross in the '40s and

Tim Russell. was a member of the Wexford County team that made the break-through in the early '50s. He retired in '53 and became a selector in '54. He was a lovely sweet hurler who could score points from very difficult angles but it was his knowledge of the game and his ability to pass it on to others that later made him a very good mentor.

OLIVER GOUGH

One of the best ball-players of his time, Oliver Gough first came into the Wexford team for the replay of the Leinster final in 1955. He was Kilkenny born and reared and had come to work in County Wexford and joined the Ferns hurling club. Just twenty years old, he won his place on the county team after giving the finest

Oliver Gough.

exhibition of hurling I have ever seen in the Wexford championship. His best display in the Wexford jersey was in New York in 1957. He also played a great game at left half forward when we beat Limerick in the league final of 1958 and some years later played a few games for his native Kilkenny.

THE PLAYERS WHO MISSED OUT

The Wexford teams of the late forties and early fifties had some brilliant individual players who never won an All Ireland medal. Some were unlucky. Martin Byrne, Tim Russell and Sam 'Wilkie' Thorpe all contributed greatly to the building of the team, but age ruled them out before the big breakthrough. John Cummins of Horeswood was playing

John Cummins who emigrated in 1953.

great hurling at centre forward, but he emigrated in 1953. He was big and forceful with lots of skill in a style very similar to Nickey Rackard. If he had been available in '54 I think we would have won three in a row. Martin Flood too played several games for the county in the early fifties but never once in his best position, which was centre field. He was a leader and always inspirational when playing with his club. He deserved an All-Ireland medal. The most skilful hurler in Wexford in the '50s was Harry O'Connor of the Enniscorthy St Aidan's Club. He made a few appearances with the county team but failed to produce his club form, which was a great pity.

KEVIN SHEEHAN

Kevin Sheehan, who was the official trainer of the team, got very little recognition for his work. Because of the lifestyle in the fifties, most players didn't need the type of training that is needed today. Being a great athlete himself, Kevin knew when players were fit enough to play a game of hurling. All our training was

Kevin Sheehan.

done with a hurl in our hands. Kevin Sheehan was an international class athlete but in the early '40s when he was at the height of his career, there were no International Athletic Meetings because of World War II. He was Irish 120yd hurdles Champion in 1944 and won the championships at high jump and cross country also. We had no scientific way of measuring our fitness levels in the fifties, but Kevin could tell you when you needed to do a little more.

THE MANAGEMENT

In the '50s there was no manager of the county senior hurling team. Five selectors were appointed by the County Board and they selected and managed the team. Meetings of the selectors were chaired by Sean Browne who was County Board Chairman. The men who selected the team in '55-'56 were Patsy Boggan of the St Martin's club, Piercestown, Tim Russell of New Ross, Peter Hayes of St Aidan's, Enniscorthy, Nick Bowe of Horeswood and Nickey Rackard of Rathnure. Early in the '50s Tom Kehoe of New Ross, Mikie Redmond of Rathnure, Eamonn Cullen of Cloughbawn, John Canavan of St Aidan's, Jim Walsh of St Martin's and Tom Butler of Adamstown were selectors.

THE BAG MAN

The 'bag man' was a great character from Enniscorthy by the name of Bill Peare. He got this name because his job was to take care of the jerseys and the spare hurls which he carried in two big canvas bags. On the day of a big game Bill was the busiest man about. He would check to make sure each player was properly togged out and had the correct number on his back. When the game was over he stood at the dressing room door keeping out "intruders". Men like Bill Peare seldom get credit for the kind of work they do and sometimes get roped into doing jobs for which they are not very well qualified.

In the early '50s the rule was that each participating county would supply a lines-man for every game they played in the National League. Being a linesman is a very thankless job, but Bill was always willing to take on the task and, as a result, we felt confident that all doubtful balls would go Wexford's way! I remember one very cold Sunday when we were playing Laois in Portlaoise and Bill was lines-man. Some of the Laois

Bill Peare, affectionately known as 'The Bagman' became as well known in Croke Park as the players.

supporters felt that a few of his decisions were questionable and were waiting for him at the gateway as we left the pitch. To the credit of the Laois players, they made sure that the Wexford players and Bill got to the safety of the dressing room. We only realised the seriousness of our situation when a rather large stone came crashing through our dressing-room window. We could now see fifty or sixty hardy looking Laois men outside shouting at us to send out the man with the cap and the kid gloves. Bill always wore a cap and on this occasion as he patrolled the side line, he was also wearing a fine pair of kid gloves belonging to one of the players. The problem was that on a couple of occasions the Laois fans booed Bill when they didn't agree with his decisions, so he turned towards them and gave them a slow handclap with his kid gloves. We weren't too worried for a while and thought these fellows outside would soon get cold and go home, but we were wrong. Instead they got more vocal and said they were not moving until they saw the man with the cap. Twenty minutes or more elapsed and we all had our clothes on and were ready to leave, but we didn't want to have a confrontation with the lads outside. A few of the lads were getting a bit impatient and said they would chance going out, but Sean Brown who was getting very annoyed by this time said "no, we'll all go together and if we have to we'll fight our way out". Now there were about thirty of us in the dressing room, but the only one the lads outside wanted to see was Bill Peare. Someone suggested a solution; we could smuggle Bill out! Jim Quinn, who was a member of the panel, had a fine new cromby overcoat and a tidy green hat. The plan was; Bill would put on this coat and hat and get out unnoticed, but there was a small problem. Jim Quinn was over six feet tall and Bill Peare was about five foot six so the coat didn't fit very well, but it was worth a try. This was the plan. Five men would leave the dressing room first to see what the reaction would be from the lads outside, then ten or twelve more of the bigger lads would leave with Bill well camouflaged in their midst. After about five minutes the remainder of us would leave and bring the bag of jerseys and anything else that was left behind. I was the last man to leave, so I gave a glance back to see if we were forgetting anything. The only thing I saw was a peaked cap on the seat in the corner of the dressing-room. I didn't go back for it. As we walked away from the dressing room a young lad brushed by us and went into the room. In a second he was out again with the cap and shouted "The little f***** is gone". We beat Laois that day but I don't think Bill Peare's performance was appreciated, he was never asked to act as lines-man again.

The next job Bill got was his favourite and the one for which he became famous. He would stand at the back of the goal into which Wexford were playing, holding Nickey Rackard's heavy hurl. Each time Nickey got a 21 yard free, Bill would dash out onto the pitch to exchange hurls with Nickey. As soon as the free was taken he was out again to repeat the exchange of hurls. If Nickey's shot was successful Bill would stop and wave to the crowd before taking up his position behind the goal again. He gave years of service to Wexford hurling through good times and bad and he will always be fondly remembered for his efforts.

JOHN D. HICKEY'S TRIBUTE

At the end of 1954, John D. Hickey, considered by many as "the greatest hurling journalist of all time", was recalling the year's most memorable sporting occasions and this is what he wrote:

"Strange it may seem, but my still very vivid recollection of my sports thrills of 1954 are tinged with no little anxiety about the future. Every time I recall the majesty of Bobby Rackard's display for Wexford in the All-Ireland hurling final against Cork, I cannot help wondering if I have seen, rather than that I am to see.

My musing takes the shape that I saw the limit of human achievement as far as defensive hurling is concerned in the performance of the 6ft 2ins boy from Killanne at Croke Park on September 5th.

Down the years I have seen scores and scores of great backs. Such was the enjoyment they brought me that I reserve the right not to list them, as mention of their names might in this instance be construed as a revision of opinion about their merits.

But not all of them combined so coursed my blood as did the Wexford man as he smashed raid after raid by Cork. Times out of number he withered onslaughts by the All-Ireland champions and, seemingly impervious to hurt, came through forests of hurleys and battalions of opponents to get in clearances of prodigious length.

Here was the anvil of hurling absorbing all Cork had to

offer and striking back again and again and again until it seemed that even such a man must weary of it all. But not a bit of it. Whether at centre half or fullback he extricated himself and his County from all manner of situations to become the talk of hurling Ireland everywhere and every time really great hurlers are the subject of discussion.

My regrets about the memorable occasion are that I fear the likes of Rackard's display may never again be seen and I am sorry I was not a Wexford man for that hour. Then you may say there would have been the pangs of defeat, but believe me, I would not have been the least distressed on that score after having seen a county man provide me with such armour did I find myself in hurling argument in any county one might care to name.

SPORTS PROFILE

STAUNCH MEN OF WEXFORD.

The poet who said: "'Tis not in mortals to command success" would have some reason to revise that opinion had he been at Croke Park last Sunday afternoon when the Wexford hurling team, bewitched, bamboozled and bedevilled for thirty minutes by the rampant Tipperary men, yet came out undaunted for the second half, and fairly and squarely conquered their seeming conquerors.

One wonders if shades from Vinegar Hill or Boolavogue were summoned to the Wexford dressing-room at half time to infuse new and unconquerable resolve into the always staunch hearts of the hurlers in purple and gold, but certain it is that, with the wind behind them, the men from the Slaney made the achievement of the impossible look relatively easy.

There were, of course, some who contributed more than others to this sensational defeat of the gallant and able Munster men but a fifteen-points lead cannot be wiped out by one man, or by ten. Such a feat can only be accomplished by a whole team, all animated by one and the same unshakeable resolve, and it was as a team that Wexford triumphed on Sunday last.

From Arty Foley in goal to Tom Dixon at the top of the left each man played his part in that glorious and amazing victory which will never be forgotten so long as ash is swung in Rathnure or Cloughbawn, in Ross or Adamstown, or Horeswood, in Camross or Enniscorthy town.

From the many defeats which they suffered in crucial league and championship games between their first uprising in 1950 and the National League final of 1955, this Wexford team has now emerged into the warm sunshine of victory and, through the past achievement to achievement, with last

Sunday's remarkable come-back a crowning glory which may well outlast, in the memories of those who watched, even their well-earned All-Ireland triumph last September.

But whether as champions or runner-up, whether in victory or defeat, these stalwart boys of Wexford have carried with them onto every field they graced a genuine spirit of sportsmanship as honest in victory as it has always been unsullied in defeat.

These players, who have, by their heart-warming displays, brought so much glory of late to the hurling fields by the Slaney, are men of might and brawn who believe in the full vigour of the game. But if they hurl hard, they hurl fairly.

And that is why no team has been more popular, not alone with their myriad of home supporters, but with hurling fans all Ireland over who appreciate courage in defeat, dignity in victory and sportsmanship, come what may.

Bobby
A Tribute to Bobby Rackard

I

Tonight we stand in memory of a great one who is gone.
Though our heads are bowed in sorrow now, great memories
linger on.
There are but few who really knew this shy and private
man.
A hurling prince, a gentle giant, Bobby Rackard from
Killanne.

II

No wonder then our sorrow when the dreaded news had
come.
But maybe God had better things for his true and faithful
son.
The legacy you left behind lives on in Wexford still.
When hurling men with heads held high go marching by
the Hill.

III

Though the years have passed great memories last and we
think of '54.
I see you still like Blackstairs Hill you stood in front of
Goal.
When Ring and Co. came rushing through like torrents
from the Lee
With cap pulled low you stole the show your courage was
the key.

(Continued on Page 267)

IV

Your help for friend and neighbour makes your memory
greater yet.
Your hurling skill and will to win are things we'll not forget.
No films show, no video, but it's chiseled in the mind.
Of the privileged few, who saw and knew the best was now
behind.

V

God rest you Bobby, it's over now, tonight we'll say a prayer.
That you have found the peace you sought, on earth while
you were there.
You left the greatest milestone ever written in a scroll.
And may God in all his majesty have mercy on your soul.

By Martin Codd

Cuchulainn's Son
A Tribute to Nickey Rackard

The challenge of an ancient game
brought glory, glory to your name
though March winds blew the crowds still came
to watch you gentle hero.
In life's long march you made us proud
and many a voice from out the crowd
called out your name aloud, aloud
an echo still resounding

And Blackstairs men who saw you then
still speak of you in awe,
on Carmen's green where you had been
they tell of what they saw,
we watched you on September fields
and lightning was the drive
you were the one Cuchulainn's son in 1955.

The hand that held the stick of ash,
and the man who led with style and dash,
Oh! Carrigtwohill once felt the crash
and Bennettsbridge and Thurles,
And when in later life you beat
the devil on that lonely street
you showed us how to take defeat
with dignity and courage.

(Continued on Page 269)

The last parade was sad and slow
the last oration spoken low
and as, on green fields long ago
the Diamond stood beside you
old friend they flanked you side by side
and the tears they shed were tears of pride
an ash tree toppled when you died
and scattered seeds at random.

Tom Williams